READING FUNDAMENTALS

by Aileen Weintraub

GRADE

6

New York

New York

An Imprint of Sterling Publishing
1166 Avenue of the Americas
New York, NY 10036

ISBN 978-1-4114-7886-2

Distributed in Canada by Sterling Publishing Co., Inc.
c/o Canadian Manda Group, 165 Dufferin Street
Toronto, Ontario, Canada M6K 3H6
Distributed in the United Kingdom by GMC Distribution Services
Castle Place, 166 High Street, Lewes, East Sussex, England BN7 1XU
Distributed in Australia by Capricorn Link (Australia) Pty. Ltd.
P.O. Box 704, Windsor, NSW 2756, Australia

For information about custom editions, special sales, and premium and corporate purchases, please contact Sterling Special Sales at 800-805-5489 or specialsales@sterlingpublishing.com.

Manufactured in Canada
Lot #:
2 4 6 8 10 9 7 5 3 1
03/16

www.flashkids.com

Dear Parent,

Being able to read and understand nonfiction texts is an essential skill that not only ensures success in the classroom but also in college and beyond. Why is nonfiction reading important? For one thing, close reading of nonfiction texts helps build critical thinking skills. Another reason is nonfiction reading builds your child's background knowledge. That means your child will already have a wealth of knowledge about various subjects to build on while progressing in school. You can feel good knowing you'll be laying the foundation for future success by ensuring that your child develops the necessary skills that nonfiction reading comprehension provides.

The activities in this book are meant for your child to be able to do on his or her own. However, you can assist your child with difficult words, ideas, and questions. Reading comprehension skills take time to develop, so patience is important. After your child has completed each activity, you can go over the answers together using the answer key provided in the back of this workbook. Provide encouragement and a sense of accomplishment to your child as you go along!

Extending reading comprehension beyond this workbook is beneficial and provides your child with the opportunity to see why this skill is so essential. You might read a newspaper article together and then discuss the main ideas. Or head to the library to find a book on your child's favorite subject. Remember, reading is fun. It opens the door to imagination!

A Terra-cotta Army

For thousands of years, legends have been told of the great Chinese emperor Qin Shi Huang Di and his terra-cotta army. Terra-cotta is red clay often used to sculpt pottery and statues. It was believed that the emperor had tombs filled with jewels guarded by this stone army.

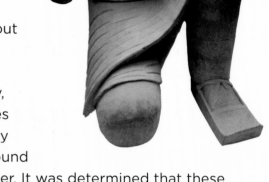

In 1974, farmers in the small town of Xi'an, China, were running out of water for their crops. It had been a hot summer, and the drought was becoming dangerous. They knew that the only way to save their fields was to dig wells deep in the earth. On the third day of digging, a farmer named Yang Zhifa hit something with his shovel. When he finally unearthed it, he realized it was a head made out of terra-cotta. With the help of others, Zhifa continued digging until he unearthed an entire statue.

As soon as archeologists heard about the discovery, they rushed to the site to investigate. They took samples of the earth to see what they could find. Soon after, they made one of the biggest discoveries of all time. They found thousands of warriors buried in an underground chamber. It was determined that these terra-cotta warriors were more than 2,000 years old. Now they had proof that the legends of Emperor Qin Shi Huang Di were true!

Along with the warriors, the archeologists also found wooden chariots, thousands of weapons, statues of life-sized horses, and even acrobats made of terra-cotta. The most amazing part was that many of the statues were still in excellent condition. The warriors were positioned in a variety of ways. Some were kneeling, others were standing, and still others were sitting. One of the most interesting findings was that each warrior had a very distinct face. This meant that special care was taken to make each warrior unique.

It is believed that the emperor built this army to protect him from invaders after his death. It took more than 700,000 men to build the army over a span of thirty-six years. Unfortunately, tomb raiders broke into the tomb to steal the emperor's treasures not long after he died. Archeologists have determined that their actions possibly caused the tomb to cave in and bury the warriors.

As of today, nearly 8,000 warriors have been found. People from all over the world come to visit the site, which has been turned into a museum. Just think, if it weren't for farmers looking for water, one of the greatest mysteries of the ancient world might still be hidden away.

1. What is terra-cotta?

   a) a type of clay   **b)** a type of liquid   **c)** a type of mineral

2. What was the name of the city where the Chinese farmers lived?

   a) Hong Kong   **b)** Xi'an   **c)** New York

3. What were the farmers running out of when they began digging in the earth?

   a) furniture   **b)** water   **c)** clothing

4. What did Yang Zhifa hit with his shovel?

   a) a rock   **b)** a vase   **c)** a terra-cotta head

5. Who came to the site to investigate?

   a) archeologists   **b)** biologists   **c)** chemists

6. Where were the warriors found?

   a) in an abandoned ship   **b)** in an underground chamber   **c)** they were never found

7. How old were the warriors?

   a) more than 2,000 years old   **b)** 500 years old   **c)** 2 million years old

8. In what kind of condition were the statues found?

   a) poor   **b)** excellent   **c)** fair

9. What was very interesting about the faces of the warriors?

   a) each one was distinct   **b)** all the faces looked the same

   c) the faces weren't finished

10. Why did the emperor build the army?

    a) to impress others   **b)** to protect him from invaders after his death

    c) no one knows why

11. Who broke into the emperor's tomb?

    a) pirates   **b)** gypsies   **c)** raiders

12. Approximately how many warriors have been found?

    a) 400   **b)** 8,000   **c)** 2,000

Living with Chimpanzees

There are many ways to study animals and their behavior. You can read about them, study them in a lab, or observe them in their natural habitat. Jane Goodall is an anthropologist who decided to do something different. She set out to live among a group of chimpanzees to see what their lives were really like.

Goodall was born in 1934, in London, England. Growing up, she enjoyed watching birds and other animals. As a young child, she knew that one day she wanted to travel to Africa to study exotic animals.

When she was old enough, Goodall saved enough money to travel to Kenya, Africa. There, she met the famous anthropologist Louis Leakey, who offered her a job. Leakey asked her to live alone with the chimpanzees in the wild. No one had ever done this before. For Goodall, it was a dream come true. She set up her camp near a group of chimpanzees in the Kakombe Valley.

Unlike most other anthropologists, Goodall didn't have formal training. This actually helped her because she developed her own unique way of recording facts and observing animals. For example, she gave the chimpanzees names. At the time, other anthropologists just assigned a number to animals they observed. Goodall named one chimpanzee Gigi and another one Flo. There was also Frodo, Mr. McGregor, Goliath, and David. It took a year for Goodall to establish enough trust for the chimpanzees to get close to her. It helped that she always offered them bananas.

Through her observations, Goodall made interesting discoveries that helped shape the course of scientific study. For example, she was the first person to realize that chimpanzees use tools. They stuck blades of grass into holes to catch and eat termites. This was an important finding because it was previously thought that only humans knew how to use tools. Goodall also discovered that chimpanzees hunted for meat. Before her observations, scientists thought they were vegetarians.

Living among the chimpanzees, Goodall quickly found that these animals have a wide range of emotions. She observed that, like humans, chimpanzees feel happy, sad, and angry. She also noticed that each chimpanzee had its own distinct personality. Some were quiet and sweet while others were much more aggressive and demanding.

Goodall spent two years living with chimpanzees. When her study was over, she dedicated the rest of her career to educating others about her findings.

Answer the questions.

1. Where was Jane Goodall born?

_____

2. As a young child, where did Goodall want to travel?

_____

3. When Goodall traveled to Kenya, who was the famous anthropologist she met?

_____

4. What did Leakey ask Goodall to do?

_____

5. Why was what Leakey asked so unusual?

_____

6. Did Goodall have formal training to be an anthropologist?

_____

7. How did not having training help her?

_____

8. What did Goodall give the chimpanzees that other anthropologists never did?

_____

9. How long did it take Goodall to establish trust with the chimpanzees?

_____

10. What did she offer the chimpanzees to help establish this trust?

_____

11. What did the chimpanzees use that no one ever realized before?

_____

12. After she left the chimpanzees, what did Goodall dedicate the rest of her life to?

_____

The Celebration of Diwali

Every year in the fall, Hindu Indians around the world light hundreds of small clay oil lamps called *diyas*. They place these lamps throughout their homes, in courtyards and gardens, and even on rooftops. This is because they are preparing for a very special holiday called *Diwali.* The word *Diwali* means "rows of light lamps." This festival of lights lasts five days and is the biggest holiday in India. It marks the celebration of the Hindu New Year.

Diwali falls on the fifteenth day of the Hindu month of Kartika. This is usually sometime in October or November. The holiday honors the Hindu goddess of wealth, Lakshmi. During this time, people who practice the Hindu religion pray to Lakshmi to bring wealth and prosperity in the coming year.

Hindus celebrate Diwali by bringing light during a dark time of the year. Along with the clay lamps, they also string up electric lights, make bonfires, and even set off fireworks. Some people keep their doors and windows open while they are celebrating to invite in Lakshmi. Another way Hindus celebrate Diwali is by drawing beautiful patterns on the ground outside their homes. They hope Lakshmi will see these patterns and want to come visit. These patterns are called *rangoli*.

Each of the five days of Diwali marks a special event. On the first day, women clean their homes and shop for new kitchen utensils. The second day is set aside for decorating. On the third day, families gather together for a huge feast, prayer, and festivities. On the fourth day, the New Year is celebrated by visiting friends and relatives with gifts and well wishes. On the last day, married sisters make a huge meal for their brothers.

Hindus celebrate Diwali for different reasons, depending on where they live in India. In the northern part of India, people celebrate King Rama's return to Ayodhya after his exile. The story says that his wife, Sita, has been kidnapped by a ten-headed demon named Ravana. Rama defeats Ravana, and the people of Ayodhya light oil lamps to guide him home.

In the southern part of India, people celebrate Diwali as the day that Lord Krishna defeated Narakasura. Narakasura was a greedy demon that raided and plundered kingdoms.

In the western part of India, Diwali is celebrated as the day that Lord Vishnu sent the evil King Bali to the underworld.

All of these stories have one important thing in common. They all mark the triumph of good over evil.

Use the words from the word bank to complete each sentence.

diyas	New Year	lights	decorating	wealth	*rangoli*
five	gifts	banished	underworld	demon	evil

1. The small clay lamps that are lit during Diwali are called _____.

2. Diwali lasts _____ days.

3. The holiday marks the Hindu _____.

4. Diwali celebrates the festival of _____.

5. The holiday honors Lakshmi, the Hindu goddess of _____.

6. Some people draw patterns on the ground called _____.

7. People visit friends and relatives to give them _____.

8. The second day of Diwali is set aside for _____.

9. In the northern part of India, people celebrate King Rama's return to Ayodhya after his father _____ him.

10. Narakasura was a greedy _____ who raided and plundered kingdoms.

11. In the western part of India, Diwali is celebrated as the day that Lord Vishnu sent the evil King Bali to the _____.

12. Diwali is a holiday that marks the triumph of good over _____.

Say Cheese!

When someone snaps a picture of you, do you smile and say, "Cheese"? Keeping your teeth healthy helps you look good when you smile. It also helps you chew food and speak clearly.

Taking care of your teeth is important so you don't get cavities. When you eat food, sugar is left over on your teeth. Bacteria attack the sugar, causing acid to build up. This bacteria is called plaque. When the plaque builds up, it sticks to your teeth. Then it begins eating away at the enamel. Enamel is the hard coating that protects your teeth. Plaque can also cause gum disease called gingivitis. This disease can cause your gums to swell, becoming red and sore.

To keep from getting cavities and gingivitis, it is a good idea to brush your teeth at least twice a day. You can brush them once in the morning and once before bedtime. You want to make sure to brush all your teeth, not just the ones in front. Reach way back and along the sides of your molars. Your molars are the thick teeth in the back of your mouth. It is easy for food to get stuck there. Don't forget to brush your tongue too. This will help keep your breath fresh. The American Dental Association suggests getting a toothbrush with soft bristles and replacing it every three to four months.

Another way to keep your teeth healthy is to use dental floss. Dental floss is a waxy string that you slip between your teeth once a day to help get rid of extra food particles and bacteria. Dental floss is important because it can get to places that your toothbrush can't.

Twice a year, make an appointment to visit your dentist. Your dentist can check for cavities, give your teeth a cleaning, and take x-rays. X-rays show what is going on underneath your gums. Dentists can also demonstrate the best way to brush and floss your teeth.

While brushing your teeth, flossing, and dental visits are all ways to keep your teeth healthy, it is also a good idea to think about the foods you eat. Sugary foods quickly break down the enamel on your teeth and cause cavities. It is better to eat fruits and vegetables and drink water instead of juice or soda.

Practice these tips and the next time someone tells you to say, "Cheese," you can smile, knowing you have bright, healthy teeth.

Read each statement. Write *true* or *false*.

1. Taking care of your teeth will help you chew your food and speak clearly. _____

2. If you brush your teeth too much, you will get cavities. _____

3. Plaque is a type of bacteria that builds up on your teeth. _____

4. Enamel is a hard coating that protects your teeth. _____

5. Gingivitis will not make the gums sore. _____

6. You have to brush your teeth only once a day. _____

7. It is difficult for food to get stuck in your molars. _____

8. Dental floss can help you get rid of extra food particles and bacteria. _____

9. The American Dental Association recommends changing your toothbrush every six months. _____

10. An x-ray can show what is going on beneath your gums. _____

11. Sugary foods do not harm your teeth. _____

12. You should visit your dentist twice a year. _____

Let's Grow Salt Crystals!

Crystals are made up of molecules that come together to form different shapes and patterns. They occur when hot liquid cools and hardens.

There are many different types of crystals. Some of the more familiar ones are sugar, salt, and ice. Other crystals, such as rubies, diamonds, and emeralds, are not as common. Those crystals are rare and are often used for jewelry. Every crystal has its own unique size and shape. This means that no two are alike.

You may be wondering how crystals are made! The answer is that it depends on the kind of crystal. In nature, certain types of rock crystals form when hot magma from a volcano cools. Snowflakes are made when water freezes. Salt crystals are made when the chemicals sodium and chlorine bond together.

The one thing that all crystals have in common is that they form through the process of evaporation. For example, when water from saltwater evaporates, salt crystals are left behind.

Let's make our own salt crystals! If we observe closely, we might see how evaporation allows crystals to form.

You will need:

❏ Water	❏ A small glass jar	❏ Half a cup of salt	❏ A pot for boiling
❏ String	❏ A pencil	❏ Food coloring	
❏ Scissors	❏ A tablespoon	❏ A teaspoon	

Step 1: Fill the pot with water and place it on the stove to boil. Make sure an adult is helping you.

Step 2: Once the water has boiled, carefully pour it into the glass jar (again, with adult help).

Step 3: Using the spoon, add 3 tablespoons of salt to the boiled water.

Step 4: Slowly stir the water and salt together until you can no longer see the salt.

Step 5: Continue to add more salt, stirring until it dissolves.

Step 6: Measure out 3 teaspoons of food coloring and pour into the mixture.

Step 7: Put the lid on the jar and make sure it is tight.

Step 8: Carefully shake the jar. Then remove the lid.

Step 9: Cut a piece of string that is long enough to hang into the water without touching the bottom of the jar.

Step 10: Tie the string around the pencil.

Step 11: Set the pencil on top of the jar and balance the string inside the water.

Step 12: Put the jar in a sunny place for at least two days. Check back to see if salt crystals appear on the string. If the crystals stop growing, add more salt.

What's the order? Number the events *1* to *12*.

1. _____ Set the pencil on top of the jar and balance the string inside the water.

2. _____ Cut a piece of string that is long enough to hang into the water without touching the bottom of the jar.

3. _____ Measure out 3 teaspoons of food coloring and pour into the mixture.

4. _____ Put the jar in a sunny place for at least two days. Check back to see if salt crystals appear on the string. If the crystals stop growing, add more salt.

5. _____ Tie the string around the pencil.

6. _____ Carefully shake the jar. Then remove the lid.

7. _____ Slowly stir the water and salt together until you can no longer see the salt.

8. _____ Continue to add more salt, stirring until it dissolves.

9. _____ Fill the pot with water and place it on the stove to boil. Make sure an adult is helping you.

10. _____ Using the spoon, add 3 tablespoons of salt to the boiled water.

11. _____ Put the lid on the jar and make sure it is tight.

12. _____ Once the water has boiled, carefully pour it into the glass jar (again, with adult help).

The Mystery of the *Mona Lisa*

Would you believe that there is a painting so famous it hangs behind bulletproof glass? The *Mona Lisa* is an oil painting by Italian Renaissance artist Leonardo Da Vinci. The word *Renaissance* means "rebirth." This was a time of great cultural change in Italy. Da Vinci became well known for his fresh approach to art. Many of his paintings include a lot of detail, especially the *Mona Lisa*. This painting is considered the most famous painting in the world.

The *Mona Lisa* has been hanging in the Louvre museum in Paris, France, since 1797. It is so well known, that more than 9 million people a year visit the Louvre just to see it. There are even special guards who are assigned to make sure the painting stays safe.

Part of why the painting is so famous is because it is shrouded in mystery. For centuries, no one was sure why this picture was painted or who commissioned it. When a piece of art is commissioned, it means that it was special ordered for a certain purpose. It was not even entirely clear who the person in the painting was! Art historians also wondered how long Da Vinci worked on the painting. What we did know is that whoever commissioned the painting never received it. Instead, it ended up in the French royal collection. No one is even sure how it got there.

Historians have studied this painting for centuries to solve the mystery. It is now believed that the *Mona Lisa* is the portrait of a merchant's wife named Lisa Gherardini. It is possible that the painting was commissioned to celebrate the purchase of the couple's new home. Another theory is that it was commissioned to celebrate the birth of their second son. Given the period of these events, it is now believed Da Vinci painted the *Mona Lisa* between 1503 and 1506.

Another big mystery about the *Mona Lisa* is her smile. Historians wonder what she finds so amusing. Some believe Da Vinci painted a half smile to represents the idea of happiness. Others believe she is smiling because she has a secret.

Over the years, the painting has been vandalized and even stolen. In 1911, an employee at the Louvre stole the painting and tried to sell it in Italy. In 1956, someone threw acid on the painting. That same year someone else threw a rock at it. Each time, the painting had to be repaired. This is why great care is taken to protect this timeless masterpiece.

Read each question and circle the correct answer.

1. What kind of painting is the *Mona Lisa*?

   a) oil   b) charcoal   c) print

2. What was the name of the artist who painted the *Mona Lisa*?

   a) Andy Warhol   b) Leonardo Da Vinci   c) Galileo

3. What does the word *Renaissance* mean?

   a) awakening   b) darkness   c) rebirth

4. About how many people view the *Mona Lisa* each year?

   a) too few to count   b) 9 million   c) 600

5. In which museum can one visit the *Mona Lisa*?

   a) the Louvre   b) the Metropolitan   c) the Tower of London

6. Where is the museum where the *Mona Lisa* hangs?

   a) Paris, France   b) Florence, Italy   c) London, England

7. What does the word *commission* mean?

   a) to get for free   b) to paint many copies   c) to specially order artwork

8. Who do historians now believe the *Mona Lisa* is?

   a) a merchant's wife   b) a fisherman's wife   c) a tailor

9. When did Da Vinci paint the *Mona Lisa*?

   a) between 1704 and 1706   b) between 1503 and 1506   c) between 1603 and 1606

10. What do some historians believe the *Mona Lisa*'s smile represents?

   a) happiness   b) pain   c) a joke

11. Who tried to steal the painting in 1911?

   a) a museum visitor   b) a museum employee   c) another artist

12. In 1956, what was thrown at the painting?

   a) a rock and paint   b) acid and a ball   c) acid and a rock

Water, Wind, and Ice

Have you ever wondered how mountains and valleys are formed? Maybe you've watched a stream after a rainstorm and wondered why it was so muddy. The answer to these questions can be found if we study erosion. Erosion occurs when water, wind, or ice wears away the surface of Earth.

Water Erosion

Moving water is the most common form of erosion. Heavy rain carries away small fragments of rock and mud. As streams and rivers flow downstream, their banks are worn away. Over millions of years, this erosion can create large valleys. An example is the Colorado River in Arizona. For more than 5 million years, this river has been carving a canyon deep into the earth. Maybe you've heard of it. It is called the Grand Canyon. Due to erosion, the canyon is an average of 1 mile (1.6 km) deep and up to 18 miles (29 km) wide.

Water also causes erosions on coastlines. As waves crash against the shore, they crush nearby rocks. Over time, these rocks are broken down into pebbles. The pebbles further erode until they turn to sand. Ocean waves can carry the sand out to sea, causing the coastline to move farther inland as the beach erodes.

Wind Erosion

Strong winds cause erosion by carrying dust, sand, and volcanic ashes to other places. Examples of wind erosion can be seen in the sand dunes of the Sahara. Dunes form when wind blows sand against an obstacle. The obstacle can be a tree, a bush, or even a rock. Since the sand can't get past the obstacle, it begins to pile up. Some of these sand dunes are more than 1,000 feet (300 m) high!

In dry regions, wind blasts sand against rocks, causing the rocks to wear away. This also makes the rocks smooth and polished. Wind erosion is so powerful it can wear away an entire mountain range over time. This happened in Central Australia. Today, all that is left is a sandstone rock formation called Ayers Rock.

Ice Erosion

Slow-moving glaciers cause erosion by traveling downhill and across land. As these huge masses of ice move, they collect rocks and sand. The rocks and sand rub against the earth as they travel with the glacier. The glaciers are so massive that they carve out basins and form valleys as they move. Would you believe that glaciers are responsible for carving out the land we live on? This occurred during a period called the ice age, when huge glaciers moved across the continents. Today, in places such as Antarctica, glaciers continue to cause erosion.

Read each phrase. Mark if it is referring to water, wind, or ice erosion.

	Water	Wind	Ice
1. the most common form of erosion			
2. caused by slow-moving glaciers			
3. blasts sand against rocks, causing the rocks to wear away			
4. cause erosion by traveling downhill and across land			
5. caused a sandstone rock formation called Ayers Rock			
6. carved a canyon deep in the earth			
7. erodes coastlines by crushing nearby rocks			
8. responsible for carving out the land we live on			
9. created sand dunes in the Sahara			
10. carries away small fragments of rock and mud			
11. continues to cause erosion in places such as Antarctica			
12. makes rocks smooth and polished			

Kindness and Compassion

Buddhism is a religion that follows the teachings of a man named Siddhartha Gautama. Siddhartha was a wealthy prince born in India around 563 BCE. He grew up surrounded by luxury but eventually realized that possessions weren't important. When he was twenty-nine, he decided to give up all his possessions to search for peace and understanding in the world. He even gave up his royal title to become a monk. After many years of searching, Siddhartha developed his own belief system. More and more people began listening to his ideas. These followers started calling Siddhartha "the Buddha," which means "enlightened one."

Buddhism is not based on the concept of God. Instead, the main idea of Buddhism is to relieve suffering. Buddhists are nonviolent and encourage kindness and compassion. They also spend time meditating. This is the practice of sitting quietly and clearing one's mind of any thoughts. They believe that meditating helps a person come closer to finding the true meaning of life.

Buddha's teachings are known as the dharma. The dharma teaches that people are born again after they die. This cycle is called reincarnation. A person's actions in one life follow over to the next life. This means that if a person is kind and giving, he or she will be rewarded in the next life. If a person has behaved badly, the next life will be more difficult. Buddhists believe that leading a spiritual life will help them reach a state of nirvana, or enlightenment. Nirvana is the highest form of peace and happiness. Reaching nirvana allows a person to break the cycle of life and death, becoming a fully enlightened being.

People who practice Buddhism can worship anywhere they choose. However, there are two main types of temples. One is called a pagoda and the other is a stupa. A pagoda is a narrow structure with many levels, and a stupa is in the shape of a large mound. The practice of worshipping in Buddhism is called *puja*. This can include meditating, bowing, chanting, and making offerings.

When the Buddha died, his teachings were written down in a book called *Tripitaka*, meaning the three baskets. Today, nearly 500 million people around the world practice Buddhism. Most of these people live in Tibet and other parts of Asia.

Answer the questions.

1. Where was Siddhartha Gautama born?

_____

2. What did Gautama's followers call him?

_____

3. What does the term *Buddha* mean?

_____

4. What is the main idea of Buddhism?

_____

5. What is the highest form of peace and happiness called?

_____

6. What are Buddha's teachings known as?

_____

7. What is reincarnation?

_____

8. According to Buddhism, if a person is kind in this life, what will happen in the next life?

_____

9. What do Buddhists encourage?

_____

10. What is the practice of sitting quietly and clearing one's mind called?

_____

11. What are the two types of Buddhist temples?

_____

12. What is the Buddhist practice of worship called?

_____

Greenhouse Gases and Global Warming

Have you ever walked through a greenhouse? If you have, you may remember that it was pretty warm inside. The reason for this is because greenhouses are made of glass. This special design is meant to trap heat and warmth inside even if the temperature is frigid outside. Trapping the heat helps keep the plants in the greenhouse lush year-round.

Earth's atmosphere is similar to that of a greenhouse. The atmosphere is made up of different types of gases. These gases act like blankets, wrapping themselves around our planet. By doing this, they trap the sun's energy so it cannot escape, just like a greenhouse traps warmth inside its glass walls. This process is called the Greenhouse Effect.

There are many different kinds of greenhouse gases in Earth's atmosphere. They include carbon dioxide, methane, ozone, nitrous oxide, and water vapor. Some of these gases are present in only small amounts. Even so, all of the gases must act together to maintain a delicate balance. If one of these gases changes, it can affect the temperature of the entire planet. Too many greenhouse gases can cause temperatures to rise very high.

Humans produce greenhouse gases in a variety of ways. Burning fossil fuels such as coal or natural gas releases carbon dioxide. Driving a car or using electricity is another way carbon dioxide is released into the atmosphere. Chlorofluorocarbon is a type of gas released when factories make foam plastic or when we use spray cans such as hairspray. When these additional gases are released into the atmosphere, the temperature of Earth rises. This is known as global warming.

Over time, global warming will mean that summers and winters will become much hotter. This may sound okay at first, but remember, the temperature of Earth is perfect for all living things. If the climate gets too hot, glaciers will start to melt and oceans will rise. This might cause flooding in towns and cities that are near coastlines. Animals would be affected too. They would be forced to travel to cooler spots. This means that other animals might have trouble hunting prey. Scientists also believe that global warming will cause extreme weather conditions, such as powerful hurricanes or long periods of droughts. In turn, this would hurt the crops we grow for food.

These climate changes are an important issue that scientists are continuing to study. They are hoping to come up with ways to slow down global warming and reduce greenhouse gases.

Circle the correct word to complete each sentence.

1. Greenhouses are made of _____ (glass/metal).

2. Earth's atmosphere is similar to that of a _____ (moon/greenhouse).

3. The atmosphere is made up of different types of _____ (gases/methane).

4. Some greenhouse gases are present in _____ (unknown/small) amounts.

5. Too many greenhouse gases can cause temperatures to _____ (rise/fall).

6. Burning fossil fuels such as coal or natural gas releases _____ (carbon dioxide/ozone).

7. When the temperature of Earth rises, this is known as _____ (chlorofluorocarbon/global warming).

8. Global warming means that summers and winters will become _____ (cooler/hotter).

9. If the climate gets too hot, glaciers will start to _____ (melt/multiply).

10. Global warming can cause extreme _____ (soil/weather) conditions.

11. Scientists believe that global warming could cause powerful _____ (meteor showers/hurricanes).

12. Extreme droughts and hurricanes can affect the _____ (crops/livestock) we grow for food.

The Mystery of the Great Sphinx

What has the body of a lion, has the head of a human, and is made entirely of stone? It's the Great Sphinx! This sculpture is one of the most important symbols of ancient Egypt. Carved out of one huge piece of limestone, it is 240 feet (73 m) long and 66 feet (20 m) high! The Sphinx is truly massive, and why it was carved is a complete mystery.

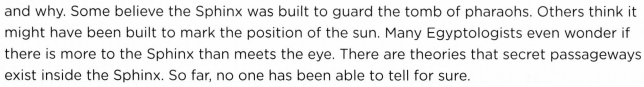

Archeologists who study ancient Egypt are called Egyptologists. These scientists have spent a lot of time studying the Sphinx to learn more about who built it and why. Some believe the Sphinx was built to guard the tomb of pharaohs. Others think it might have been built to mark the position of the sun. Many Egyptologists even wonder if there is more to the Sphinx than meets the eye. There are theories that secret passageways exist inside the Sphinx. So far, no one has been able to tell for sure.

The Sphinx is located on the Giza Plateau, bordering the Sahara Desert. It sits in a shallow trench in front of the famous Egyptian pyramids. Many Egyptologists believe that the Sphinx was built around the year 2500 BCE for a pharaoh named Khafre. Egyptologists have found that the Sphinx has been eroded by water, which is very rare in the Sahara. Thousands of years before Khafre ruled, the Sahara was thought to have experienced long periods of flooding. This could mean that the Sphinx was built much earlier than 2500 BCE. There are no inscriptions on the Sphinx to give Egyptologists clues, so they have to come up with their own conclusions.

Sand, wind, and sun have also greatly eroded the Sphinx over time. As a matter of fact, by the 1800s, it was buried up to its neck in sand. It wasn't until 1925 that a French engineer was able to remove the sand to reveal its base. Once this was done, Egyptologists could see evidence that the Sphinx was once painted in bright colors. Not only has the paint long since faded, but also many parts of the sculpture have chipped away. A long braided beard is now almost completely gone except for small fragments. Part of the traditional headdress has fallen off and the nose is missing.

Today, Egyptologists continue to try to find ways to repair the Sphinx and uncover its mysteries. Maybe one day we will find out its true origins.

Read each statement. Write *true* or *false*.

1. The Great Sphinx is one of the most important symbols of ancient Egypt. _____

2. The Sphinx is carved out of sandstone. _____

3. The Sphinx is 240 feet (73 m) long and 66 feet (20 m) high. _____

4. Archeologists who study ancient Egypt are called Egyptologists. _____

5. Many Egyptologists believe that the Sphinx was built for a pharoah's servant. _____

6. Secret passageways have been found inside the Sphinx. _____

7. Water erosion is very rare in the Sahara. _____

8. There are no inscriptions on the Sphinx to give Egyptologists clues. _____

9. Until the 1800s the Sphinx was completely buried underneath sand. _____

10. Sand, wind, and sun have eroded the Sphinx. _____

11. The Sphinx was once painted in bright colors. _____

12. The Sphinx's entire headdress has fallen off. _____

Rights and Responsibilities of Citizens

A citizen is a person who lives in a community, state, or nation. To be a U.S. citizen a person is either born in this country or has gone through certain steps to obtain citizenship. In the United States, citizens can be any race, religion, or national origin. What we all have in common is our belief in freedom and equality. As citizens, we have certain rights and privileges. Many of these rights are explained in the Bill of Rights, written by our founding fathers in 1791. Some of these include the right to free speech, the right to a fair and speedy trial, the right to worship as we choose, and the right to petition the government.

The right to vote is one of the most important rights of a citizen. Voting ensures that people have a say in who is elected to their government. Citizens also have the right to run for office. If they are elected, they can help create laws that will serve their community. With these rights come important responsibilities.

As citizens, it is our responsibility to obey the laws of our nation. Laws are rules that the government creates to protect all individuals. If a person breaks the law, there are consequences. The consequences depend on what type of crime was committed. Every nation needs laws to make sure that the rights of all citizens are respected.

Another responsibility citizens have is that they must pay taxes on their wages. A tax is money given to the government to pay for things such as road maintenance, schools, police officers, and firefighters. There are many different types of taxes. There are federal taxes, state taxes, property taxes, excise taxes, and sales tax. Each tax pays for a different program or service.

In the United States, citizens have a right to trial by a jury of peers. This means that it is also a citizen's responsibility to serve on a jury. Almost any American over the age of eighteen can be called for jury duty. If a person is called, he or she must take time off from work or school to participate in a trial. Citizens must also serve as witnesses in a trial if called to do so.

Being a good citizen means following the laws set forth by the government. In turn, being a citizen grants you many rights.

Read each phrase. Check whether it is a right or a responsibility.

	Right	Responsibility
1. Free speech		
2. Voting		
3. Following the law		
4. Paying taxes on wages		
5. Worshipping the way we want to		
6. Having a trial by jury		
7. Paying property taxes		
8. Being allowed to run for office		
9. Having a fair and speedy trial		
10. Serving on jury duty		
11. Serving as a witness in a trial		
12. Petitioning the government		

The Father of Modern Science

Galileo Galilei was born in Pisa, Italy, in 1564, during the Italian Renaissance. This was a time when people became interested in developing arts and culture. Galileo was one of six children and his father was a well-known musician. In 1574, when Galileo was ten years old, he moved to the city of Florence with his family. Here, he began to study at the Camaldolese monastery. In 1581, he went back to Pisa to study medicine at the university. While there, he developed a love for math and science. In 1585, Galileo left the university to study math.

In 1588, Galileo applied for a job as a math teacher, but no one would hire him. He continued to study and soon began giving lectures. A year later, in 1589, Galileo was offered a job at his old school, the University of Pisa. While teaching, he also began conducting experiments about motion and gravity. According to legend, one of his experiments involved dropping balls of different weights from the top of the Leaning Tower of Pisa. He proved that the rate at which a ball drops has nothing to do with its weight. Many of the people Galileo worked with disagreed with his findings. They did not like his approach to science. In 1592, he found a new job as a math teacher at the University of Padua.

In 1609, Galileo heard about a new invention. It was an instrument that could make far-away objects appear closer. He decided he was going to re-create this spyglass using eyeglass lenses. Others had made similar spyglasses, but what set Galileo's apart was that he continuously improved it. Galileo's telescope was so successful that he was offered the job of Chief Mathematician at the University of Pisa.

Galileo used his telescope to observe the stars and planets. In 1610, he discovered that four moons revolved around Jupiter. He was also able to find stars that no one even knew existed. After much research, Galileo came to the conclusion that Earth was a planet that revolved around the sun. In 1632, he even wrote a book about it. Unfortunately, the Catholic Church did not agree with Galileo and decided to arrest him.

Galileo died in 1642. In 1992, the Catholic pope expressed regrets about Galileo's arrest. Of course, Galileo's discoveries were correct, and today he is known as the father of modern science.

Complete the timeline with the correct dates.

1. _____ Galileo Galilei was born in Pisa, Italy.

2. _____ When Galileo was ten years old, he moved to the city of Florence with his family.

3. _____ He went back to Pisa to study medicine at the university.

4. _____ Galileo left the university to study math.

5. _____ Galileo applied for a job as a math teacher, but no one would hire him.

6. _____ Galileo was offered a job at his old school, the University of Pisa.

7. _____ He found a new job as a math teacher at the University of Padua.

8. _____ Galileo heard about a new invention.

9. _____ He discovered that four moons revolved around Jupiter.

10. _____ He wrote a book.

11. _____ Galileo died.

12. _____ The Catholic pope expressed regrets about Galileo's arrest.

Traveling Through Space

Do you ever look up at the stars and wonder what it would be like to travel through space? Astronauts do it all the time, but it takes a lot of preparation.

First, astronauts need to gear up! They wear protective suits made up of many layers. These space suits help keep the astronauts' temperature stable and protect them from radiation. The suits are pressurized, meaning they are filled with oxygen to help the astronauts breathe.

Once an astronaut steps out into space, he or she is in danger of floating away. To prevent this from happening, cords connect the astronaut to the spacecraft. There may also be special handrails for holding on, and sometimes an astronaut may even have the aid of a robotic arm.

Just like us, astronauts get hungry after a long day. Luckily, they get food deliveries from automated spacecrafts. These deliveries include fresh fruit, water, and freeze-dried meals. Astronauts can even preplan their menu before they head to space. Much of the food is dehydrated, meaning that the water has been removed. The astronaut has to add hot water to the food before it is ready to eat. Like us, they have ovens to cook their food. They also have coffee, tea, and juice. They are asked to record their food to make sure they are getting enough calories. This information is sent back to experts on Earth who advise them about how to stay healthy while on a mission.

Once an astronaut's day is over, they must find a place to sleep. Sleeping in space is not like sleeping at home. Everything is weightless, and there is nothing to keep the astronauts from floating around. An astronaut might have to attach his sleeping bag to a wall to make sure he or she doesn't bump into other objects. It is also not always clear when it is time to sleep. At the International Space Station, where many astronauts live while in space, there are sixteen sunsets and sunrises every day! When to sleep and when to wake up can get confusing. Astronauts stick to a schedule of sleeping for eight hours at the end of their shift. They often wear eye masks or close their window shades to keep out light from inside the space station. Before going to sleep, astronauts must make sure their space is well ventilated and has plenty of oxygen to last a full eight hours. But not everything is different in space. Before bed, astronauts might choose to listen to music, read, or use their laptops. Would you like to go on a space mission?

Read each question and circle the correct answer.

1. How many layers is an astronaut's space suit?

   a) one   b) many   c) none

2. What does the space suit protect an astronaut from?

   a) radiation   b) oxygen   c) nitrogen

3. What does the space suit do to the astronaut's temperature?

   a) keeps it unstable   b) nothing   c) keeps it stable

4. What can happen when an astronaut steps out into space?

   a) The astronaut can float away.   b) The astronaut can walk just fine.

   c) The astronaut can fall to Earth.

5. Why does an astronaut attach cords to his or her suit?

   a) to communicate with other astronauts   b) to keep from floating away

   c) to make calls home

6. What does the word *dehydrated* mean?

   a) to remove water   b) to add water   c) to drink

7. What do astronauts use to cook their food?

   a) ovens   b) special machines   c) They don't cook their food.

8. Why are astronauts asked to keep a record of the food they eat?

   a) so they don't eat too much   b) to make sure they are getting enough calories

   c) They aren't asked to record their food.

9. Why is sleeping in space different from sleeping at home?

   a) In space, everything is weightless.   b) There is no difference.

   c) There is no place to sleep in space.

10. How many sunrises and sunsets are there each day at the International Space Station?

    a) 4   b) 6   c) 16

11. When do astronauts try to get some sleep?

    a) at the beginning of their shift   b) at the end of their shift

    c) in the middle of their shift

12. What must astronauts do before going to sleep?

    a) make sure their space is well ventilated   b) call home

    c) release all the oxygen from the aircraft

Let's Get Fit

Do you like playing ball with friends, dancing, or practicing karate? You're probably having too much fun to realize it, but when you do these activities you're getting exercise. Staying active is important for every single part of your body.

Your heart is an organ made of muscles. The best way to keep this muscle strong is to do aerobic exercise. This is a type of exercise that helps your heart pump blood. It also helps deliver oxygen to the rest of your body. When you do aerobic exercise you breathe faster, your heart beats faster, and your body sweats. It may sound like hard work, but if you like to play tag or run around the soccer field you're already getting aerobic exercise. Other really good aerobic exercises include riding a bike, ice-skating, and swimming.

Strengthening your muscles is another way to stay fit. Strong muscles make your body powerful and help you lift heavy objects. Some fun ways to keep your muscles strong are to play tug-of-war, do pushups, or go to the park and do pull-ups on the high bars.

Did you know exercise is also good for your bones and helps you stay flexible, too? When you exercise you stand taller and your bones become stronger. It is also much easier to stretch and bend. As we get older, if we don't exercise, our muscles tighten and it becomes hard to do simple tasks like touch our toes. Ways to stay flexible include yoga, gymnastics, and martial arts.

The best part about exercise is that it is good for your brain. Getting out of the house and running around with friends can put you in a better mood. When you exercise, your brain releases a certain chemical known as endorphins. These endorphins actually make you happier! Exercise gives you a lot of energy, helps you sleep better at night, and can even help you get better grades. The reason for this is because when you get your blood flowing, your brain gets more oxygen. Exercise even has long-term benefits. The more exercise you do, the less likely you are to get sick. This is because exercise strengthens your immune system. Having an active lifestyle helps prevent diseases like high blood pressure and diabetes later in life.

Exercise keeps your body and mind strong. So what are you waiting for? Get out there, have some fun, and get fit!

Answer the questions.

1. What is the best type of exercise to keep your heart strong?

_____

2. What are three things that happen to your body when you do aerobic exercise?

_____

3. Name three types of aerobic exercise.

_____

4. What does having strong muscles help you do?

_____

5. List three ways to help keep your muscles strong.

_____

6. What happens to your bones when you exercise?

_____

7. As we get older, if we don't exercise, what happens to our muscles?

_____

8. What are three ways to stay flexible?

_____

9. What can getting out of the house and running around with friends do?

_____

10. What is the name of the chemical that is released when you exercise?

_____

11. What do endorphins do?

_____

12. What does having an active lifestyle help prevent later in life?

_____

The Jewish New Year

"L' shana tova!" That is what Jewish people say on Rosh Hashanah. It means "For a good year." Rosh Hashanah is the Jewish New Year. This holiday begins at sundown and lasts for two full days. It can fall anytime between the month of September and October. Unlike New Year's Eve, this new year is a quiet celebration that involves going to a Jewish temple, called a synagogue, to pray. Jews remember the creation of the world and are judged by God on this day. Rosh Hashanah is one of the holiest days of the year for Jews. Because of this, it is considered a High Holy Day.

The weeks leading up to Rosh Hashanah are a time for reflection. People may think about any wrongdoing they have committed over the past year. They may contact others to apologize for their behavior or pray for forgiveness. They may also make a vow with themselves to do better in the coming year.

When Rosh Hashanah arrives, people take off from work and many don't use electricity or drive their cars. People attend synagogue for most of the day and pray using special prayer books. In the middle of the service, a special horn called a *shofar* is blown. The *shofar* is most often made from the horn of a ram and is blown 100 times on each of the two days. When it is blown, the *shofar* sounds like wailing or crying. This is meant to remind Jews to make positive changes in their lives.

A tradition associated with this holiday is called *Tashlich*. This is when a Jewish person goes to a body of water, such as an ocean or a river, to cast off his or her sins. The person says a prayer and throws pieces of bread into the water. The bread represents the person's sins. As the bread floats away, his or her sins for the past year are cast off.

After attending a synagogue, friends and family gather for a huge meal together. A type of bread called challah is served. This bread is braided and shaped into a circle to represent eternal life before it is baked. Along with challah, apples are also served. Both are dipped in honey and passed around the table to represent a sweet new year. At the end of the meal, sweets such as honey cake or apple cake are served.

Use the words from the work bank to complete each sentence.

Bread	synagogue	circle	*Tashlich*	Rosh Hashanah	*Shofar*
work	forgiveness	reflection	world	L' Shanah Tova	100

1. _____ means "for a good year."

2. A _____ is a Jewish temple.

3. Jews remember the creation of the _____ on Rosh Hashanah.

4. _____ is considered one of the holiest days of the year.

5. The weeks leading up to this holiday are a time for _____.

6. People pray for _____.

7. People are not supposed to _____ on Rosh Hashanah.

8. _____ is a special horn that is blown.

9. The shofar is blown _____ times.

10. _____ is a tradition associated with Rosh Hashanah.

11. _____ is the type of food that is thrown into the water to cast off sins.

12. Challah is made into a _____ shape before it is baked.

Shaking Things Up

An earthquake is Earth's way of getting rid of stress. Every year, more than a million earthquakes happen throughout the world. Some are so small that most people can't feel them at all. Others can be very powerful, causing a lot of damage. Earthquakes are usually over in less than one minute, but there is no way to predict when they are coming or how strong they will be.

Earthquakes occur when plates beneath Earth's surface slide past one another. This moving and pushing puts stress on Earth's crust. After a while, the force causes the crust to break apart to relieve the pressure. The theory, or idea, that these plates slide, glide, and crash into one another causing earthquakes is known as plate tectonics.

An earthquake is strongest at its epicenter. This is the point directly above the source of the earthquake. The earthquake begins at the epicenter and then travels outward, causing seismic waves. Seismic waves are waves of energy that are caused from the breaking of rock inside Earth's crust.

Many earthquakes happen along fault lines. A fault line is a long fracture or split in Earth's crust. The San Andreas Fault in California is the boundary between two major plates that slide past each other. It is about 800 miles (1,287.5 km) long and is responsible for many earthquakes. The biggest earthquake along this fault occurred in 1906 and measured 7.7 on the Richter scale. This is a scale that scientists use to measure the force

of earthquakes. An earthquake with a rating of 1 is so tiny that you can hardly feel it. However, an earthquake with a rating of 2 is ten times stronger than an earthquake with a rating of 1. If an earthquake is rated 5 on the Richter scale, it will likely cause items to fall off a shelf and maybe break some windows. A rating of 6 might cause furniture to move around. An earthquake rated 8 or above can cause buildings to fall down.

Many earthquakes happen beneath the ocean floor. Most people never know about them because most of these quakes just cause a small ripple of waves. Occasionally, the force of an earthquake is so huge that it causes one giant wave called a tsunami. When a tsunami hits a shore, it can cause great destruction, destroying everything and everyone in its path.

Read each question and circle the correct answer.

1. How long do earthquakes usually last?

   a) less than an hour   b) less than a minute   c) fifteen minutes

2. Earthquakes occur when plates beneath Earth's surface do what?

   a) slide past one another   b) stay still   c) multiply

3. What does the moving and pushing do to Earth's crust?

   a) It doesn't affect it.   b) relieves the pressure   c) puts stress on it

4. What does the word *theory* mean?

   a) idea   b) fact   c) earthquake

5. The idea that plates slide, glide, and crash into one another is called what?

   a) tsunami   b) plate tectonics   c) Richter

6. What is the point directly above the center of an earthquake called?

   a) seismic   b) wave   c) epicenter

7. What is the term for the waves caused by the breaking apart of the rocks inside Earth's crust?

   a) seismic   b) epic   c) tsunami

8. Where is the San Andreas Fault located?

   a) Chicago   b) Australia   c) California

9. How long is the San Andreas Fault?

   a) 800 miles   b) 300 miles   c) 15 miles

10. What is the name of the scale scientists use to measure earthquakes?

    a) Williams   b) Richter   c) Andreas

11. An earthquake with a Richter scale rating of 8 or above can cause what to happen?

    a) a small tremor   b) buildings to fall   c) nothing at all

12. What is a tsunami?

    a) a giant wave   b) a plate   c) a piece of crust

The Invention of Writing

Writing is a form of communication that many of us take for granted. This is because as long as we can remember, the alphabet has always been around. But have you ever wondered how writing was invented in the first place?

It is believed that the Sumerians of ancient Mesopotamia were the first people to develop writing, in 3000 BCE. They didn't write using letters like we do today. Instead, they used signs and symbols known as cuneiform. The way cuneiform works is that each sign stands for a syllable or part of a word. This was not an easy system because remembering so many signs was very difficult for the average person. Most people during that time never even learned to write, especially women. The Sumerians had trained men called scribes whose job it was to record information.

When the Sumerians began writing, there was no such thing as paper. Fortunately, they had a lot of clay. They formed tablets out of the clay and used a reed from a river to write. If you look closely at an example of cuneiform, you might see what looks like triangles. This is because the reeds made triangular marks in the clay.

Writing was much harder and more time consuming back then, so Sumerians only wrote down very important information. Mostly, their writings included accounts of events or lists of items to be given to temples of worship. Eventually, scribes began writing down poems and stories. One of the earliest poems to have been discovered is called *The Epic of Gilgamesh*. This is a poem about a king and his many adventures. In 1700 BCE, the famous Code of Hammurabi was written in cuneiform writing. These were the first recorded laws.

It wasn't until around 1800 BCE that the Canaanite people of Northern Egypt invented the alphabet. This new alphabet was much easier to understand because it had fewer signs than cuneiform. The letters of the alphabet could be combined in various ways to make words. Now that there was a simpler way to write, more people began learning. This was good for trade and other businesses. From there, the idea of using an alphabet instead of symbols spread around the world.

Read each statement. Write *true* or *false*.

1. The Sumerians of ancient Mesopotamia invented writing. _____

2. Writing was invented in 2000 BCE. _____

3. A type of writing using signs and symbols is called cuneiform. _____

4. With cuneiform, each symbol stands for a single letter. _____

5. Cuneiform was considered difficult to learn because there
   were so many signs and symbols to remember. _____

6. Most women did not learn to write in ancient Mesopotamia. _____

7. Scribes were trained men whose job it was to record information. _____

8. The Sumerians wrote everything down on paper. _____

9. The reeds that were used for writing made square marks in the clay. _____

10. When cuneiform was first invented only very
    important information was recorded. _____

11. In 1800 BCE, the Canaanites invented the alphabet. _____

12. With the invention of the alphabet,
    it became much more difficult to write. _____

The Great Escape Artist

Can you imagine a job in which you are tied up, put in a box, and thrown into a river with only minutes to escape? It doesn't sound fun, but this is what the most famous magician in the world used to do all the time. His name was Harry Houdini!

Harry Houdini was born with the name Ehrich Weisz in Budapest, Hungary, in 1874. When he was four years old, his family moved to America. Times were tough, and Weisz and his five siblings had to help their parents by working. Weisz began shining shoes and selling newspapers. In his free time, he read books about magic.

By the time Weisz was fifteen, he knew he wanted to be a magician. First, he needed a stage name to use while performing. He had read about a famous magician named Robert-Houdin. Weisz admired this magician's work so much that he took Robert-Houdin's name, only he added the letter *i* to the end. Next he decided to use the name Harry, which was the American version of his own nickname, Ehrie.

Over the next few years, Houdini began touring around the country doing magic tricks at fairs and circuses with a partner. In 1894, he married a woman known as Bess, who became his new assistant. They wanted to do something that would set themselves apart from other magicians. One day, Houdini was invited to perform for a group of police officers in Chicago. For his act, he escaped from everything the police officers had, including handcuffs. They were so amazed, a story about Houdini's show appeared in the newspaper the next day. This news story helped launch Houdini's career. Everyone wanted to see the great escape artist.

Suddenly Houdini's shows were sold out. He began escaping from all sorts of places, including jail cells and milk cans filled with water. But it wasn't enough for Houdini. In 1907, with his hands cuffed behind his back, Houdini jumped off a bridge into a river. It was an amazing feat, but even that didn't compare to his most famous trick. It was called the Chinese Water Torture Cell. For this trick, a handcuffed and shackled Houdini was lowered headfirst into a glass box filled with water. Within minutes, he escaped.

In 1926, a student whom Houdini had invited to attend one of his shows punched him in the stomach. Houdini refused to see a doctor, continuing to perform instead. He died suddenly a few days later at the age of fifty-two.

Use the words from the word bank to complete each sentence.

five	shoes	magic	newspaper	Hungary	assistant
famous	Chicago	nickname	cuffed	fifty-two	escape artist

1. Ehrich Weisz was born in _____ .

2. Weisz had _____ siblings.

3. Weisz sold newspapers and shined _____ .

4. In his free time, he read books about _____ .

5. "Harry" was the American version of his _____ .

6. When Houdini married Bess, she became his new _____ .

7. Houdini was invited to perform for a group of police officers in _____ .

8. Houdini's act was so amazing that a story about his show appeared in a _____
   the next day.

9. He became known as the great _____ .

10. In 1907, with his hands _____ behind his back, he jumped into a river.

11. The Chinese Water Torture Cell was Houdini's most _____ trick.

12. Houdini died at the age of _____ .

Shooting Hoops

Basketball is a fun sport that helps build teamwork. James Naismith invented it in 1891 as a way to keep students busy indoors during cold winter months. The very first basketball game involved throwing a soccer ball into a peach basket that had been nailed to a railing. Since then, the sport has come a long way. Basketball can be challenging, but the rules are easy to learn. Here are the basics.

First, find a hoop. Regulation hoops are 10 feet (3 m) high, but basketball is all about making do with what you have. A standard game of basketball requires two hoops on a 94-foot-long (28.7 m) court. However, many people use one hoop to play with friends. This type of game is called half-court. If you don't have a basketball hoop, improvise. You can use a bucket or empty boxes. You will also need a basketball. If you can't find one, a similar-sized ball will do. Next, gather your friends. A full-court game requires ten players, with five on each team. If you are playing half-court, you can have three players on each team.

The way to score in basketball is to shoot the ball through the hoop. The team with the ball is called offense. The team without the ball is defense. The defense tries to steal the ball and prevent the other team from passing. When a team scores a basket, it is worth two points. The three-point line is approximately 20 feet (6.1 m) from the hoop. This means that shots taken from here are worth three points. The free-throw line is 15 feet (4.6 m) from the backboard of the hoop. Foul shots are taken from there and are worth one point each. If you are fouled while attempting to shoot, you can be awarded between one and three free throws. Fouls can occur when a player holds the ball, hits, pushes, or slaps. Once a point is scored, the ball is passed to the other team.

When you have the ball in your possession, you can take two steps without dribbling before shooting or passing the ball. Otherwise, you must be dribbling or be still with one foot on the floor. Once you stop dribbling, you cannot start again.

There are two types of passes in basketball. A chest pass is when you hold the ball at chest level and push it out without bouncing it. A bounce pass is when the ball bounces one time while being passed to a teammate.

Now that you know the basic rules, it's time to get a game going. Are you ready?

Answer the questions.

1. Who invented basketball?

_____

2. What kind of ball was used for the very first game of basketball?

_____

3. How high are regulation hoops?

_____

4. How long is a regulation court?

_____

5. When there are only three players on each team and one hoop, what type of game is being played?

_____

6. If you don't have a basketball hoop, what can you improvise with?

_____

7. How many players does a full-court game require?

_____

8. What is the team with the ball called?

_____

9. How far is the three-point line from the hoop?

_____

10. Once you stop dribbling, can you start again?

_____

11. What is the name of the pass when you are holding the ball at chest level and push it out without bouncing it?

_____

12. How many times can a ball bounce during a bounce pass?

_____

What Is a Fossil Fuel?

When people go to a gas station to fill up their car with gas, all they have to do is pull a lever. If you are cold in your home, you can turn up the heat. But have you ever wondered where the gas for a car or the heat for your home comes from?

They come from fossil fuels. Fossil fuels are decomposed plants and animals from hundreds of millions of years ago. Over time, heat and pressure within Earth's crust has turned the decayed matter into fossil fuels. Fossil fuels are responsible for more than 85 percent of the energy we use. They include oil, natural gas, and coal.

Oil is a thick black liquid found underneath the surface of Earth in between rocks. This liquid is also called petroleum and is used as fuel to power cars, vehicles, and airplanes. It can also be burned to make electricity or used to heat homes. To access the oil, refineries, or oil plants, dig deep wells in the ground and pump it into pipelines. Americans rely heavily on oil. As a nation, we use approximately 19 million barrels of oil per day.

Natural gas is made from a chemical called methane and is located just above where oil is found. It is highly flammable, meaning that it can catch fire easily. It is also invisible. It can't be smelled or seen. A smell similar to rotten eggs is added to it, so if there is a leak it can be detected. Like oil, natural gas is pumped through pipes in the ground. It is mainly used to cook food on a stove or burned to make heat.

Coal is made up of black rocks. It is used to create more than half of the electricity in the United States. Coal is found near Earth's surface in areas called coal beds. Once the coal has been taken from underground, it is loaded onto trains and transported to power plants. The power plants turn the coal into steam in order to produce electricity.

Fossil fuels are considered nonrenewable because humans cannot make them. It also takes millions of years for them to form. This means that once we use all the coal, oil, and natural gas, there won't be any left. Luckily, scientists have begun focusing on renewable sources of energy, such as solar and wind power. In the future, we will have to find ways to conserve our energy resources, while looking for new solutions.

Read each question and circle the correct answer.

1. What are fossil fuels made of?

    a) decomposed rocks   b) water   c) decomposed plants and animals

2. How old are fossil fuels?

    a) hundreds of millions of years   b) thousands of years   c) hundreds of years

3. What does heat and pressure from Earth's crust turn decayed matter into?

    a) fossil fuels   b) sand   c) water

4. What percentage of energy are fossil fuels?

    a) 75 percent   b) 85 percent   c) 90 percent

5. What is the thick, black fluid found between rocks?

    a) natural gas   b) coal   c) oil

6. What is the definition of *refinery*?

    a) an oil plant   b) powered by wind   c) underground pipes

7. Approximately how many barrels of oil per day do Americans use?

    a) 19   b) 19 million   c) 19 trillion

8. What is the chemical that natural gas is made from?

    a) propane   b) methane   c) oxygen

9. What does the word *flammable* mean?

    a) when something can easily catch fire   b) when something is fire resistant

    c) when something falls into water

10. What is the smell that is added to natural gas similar to?

    a) chocolate   b) milk   c) rotten eggs

11. Why do power plants turn coal into steam?

    a) to produce electricity   b) to make solar power   c) to power factories

12. Fossil fuels are what type of energy?

    a) renewable   b) solar   c) nonrenewable

The City-States of Ancient Greece

Ancient Greece was a civilization well known for its thoughts and ideas about government and politics. It was here that democracy was born.

In 500 BCE, ancient Greece wasn't even considered a country. It was made up of approximately 1,500 city-states. A city-state consisted of a city, along with its surrounding areas. City-states had their own leaders, made their own laws, and had their own currency. Though these city-states were close together, they were completely independent of one another and had their own ways of doing things. For example, the people of Athens were very interested in the arts and enjoyed studying science and history. The people of Sparta were a military society who raised their children to be hardy fighters. Sometimes city-states got along, but at other times they disagreed, often going to battle. A big reason for disagreement among city-states was land rights to grow food.

The people of ancient Greece were very proud of their origins. If you asked a person from the city-state of Sparta where he was from, he wouldn't say he was Greek. He would tell you he was Spartan. There were, however, certain things that united all the city-states. They worshipped the same gods, spoke the same language, and sometimes did business together, trading merchandise.

Government was a very important part of life in the city-states. Each city-state government ruled the way it thought best for its people. There were three different forms of government in ancient Greece. A monarchy or king ruled some city-states, such as Corinth. The monarchy had all the power and made all the decisions for its people. Other city-states were ruled by an oligarchy, which is a government made up of a small group. In Sparta, an oligarchy of well-respected warriors headed the government. In Athens, the people were ruled by democracy. The citizens of Athens felt that it wasn't right for one group to make all the decisions for everybody. Instead, they

elected their leaders into office and voted on new laws. Any citizen could run for office. However, not everyone in ancient Athens was considered a citizen. Women, children, and slaves had few rights, and only men over eighteen years old were allowed to vote.

The city-states of ancient Greece brought about great change in the way people live and govern. This was the birthplace of many ideas that are still used around the globe.

Draw a line to match each description to the correct term.

1. Ancient Greece was known for its thoughts and ideas about this.

2. At this time, ancient Greece was not considered a country.

3. The definition for a city and its surrounding areas in ancient Greece.

4. The people of this city-state were very interested in the arts.

5. This city-state was a military society.

6. One reason for disagreements between city-states.

7. One thing that city-states had in common.

8. The people of ancient Greece were very proud of this.

9. There were this many forms of government in ancient Greece.

10. This is another word for being ruled by a king.

11. The term for a small group of people that rules a government.

12. The type of government in which people elect leaders and vote on laws.

a) oligarchy

b) democracy

c) Athens

d) Sparta

e) land rights

f) origins

g) three

h) government

i) 500 BCE

j) city-state

k) language

l) monarchy

The Longest River

The longest river in the world winds its way through the continent of Africa for 4,160 miles (6,694.9 km). This river is so long that it flows through nine different countries, including Tanzania, Burundi, Rwanda, Democratic Republic of Congo, Uganda, Kenya, Ethiopia, Sudan, and Egypt. It is called the Nile River.

It is believed that the Nile is more than 30 million years old. The river has two main tributaries: the White Nile and the Blue Nile. Most of the water comes from the Blue Nile, which begins in Ethiopia. It is shorter than the White Nile—which starts out in Uganda—but is much more powerful. The rivers flow separately until meeting in Sudan. From there, the Nile flows all the way to the Mediterranean Sea. Unlike most rivers, this river is unique because it flows from south to north instead of north to south.

The Nile has been a source of food, transportation, and trade for the people of Africa since ancient times. Long ago, ancient Egyptians settled along the Nile because of the fertile land and lush valleys it created. They realized that the mud from the Nile River was a great natural resource for growing crops. Soon, they began building cities and temples to worship their gods nearby. They used the papyrus, a tall reed that grows in the river, to make rope, paper, cloth, and baskets. They also allowed their livestock to graze along the riverbanks.

The Egyptians watched the river closely, waiting for the floods to come. They built stone pillars called Nilometers and placed them in the river. This allowed them to measure how high the Nile rose. They knew that if it was rising too much, it would destroy their food source. If it didn't rise enough, there would be no crops to grow, and people would go hungry.

Floods from the Nile could destroy homes and communities. In ancient times, Egyptians built walls to keep out the floodwaters. By 1970, the High Aswan Dam was built to protect people from the dangerous waters. This dam is more than 12,000 feet (3,657.6 m) long and rises 364 feet (110.9 m) high. Along with the dam, an artificial lake has been created to help stem the floods. Lake Nasser stores the excess floodwater and provides Egyptians with enough water to last through the year.

Today, the Nile continues to be a life source for many communities in Africa. Tourists who are interested in experiencing the Nile can travel the river by riverboat to witness the grandness and beauty it offers.

Circle the correct word to complete each sentence.

1. The longest river in the world winds its way through the continent of _____ (Australia/Africa).

2. It is believed that the Nile is _____ (30/40) million years old.

3. The Nile has two main _____ (tributaries/banks).

4. Most of the Nile's water comes from the _____ (Blue/White) Nile.

5. The Blue Nile and the White Nile meet in _____ (Ethiopia/Sudan).

6. Ancient Egyptians settle along the Nile because of the _____ (fertile/dry) land.

7. The _____ (reeds/mud) from the Nile was a great resource for growing crops.

8. The Egyptians used _____ (papyrus/silt) to make cloth, paper, and ropes.

9. Egyptians watched the river closely to monitor _____ (floods/crocodiles).

10. Nilometers are pillars made out of _____ (metal/stone).

11. The High Aswan Dam is more than _____ (12,000 [3,657.6 m]/18,000 [5,486.4 m]) feet long.

12. Today, people can travel by _____ (steamship/riverboat) to see the beauty of the Nile.

Squares and Circles

Abstract art is the idea that paintings don't need to be about a particular subject. Rather, shapes and colors alone can tell a story. One of the most famous abstract artists was Wassily Kandinsky.

Kandinsky was born in Russia in 1866. As a child he played the cello and the piano and was fascinated by the colors found in nature. Though he was interested in music and the arts, when he grew up he studied law. One day, he went to see an art exhibit in Germany. This changed his life forever. He decided to switch careers and applied for art school.

As Kandinsky studied art, he began developing his own ideas. He felt that a painting did not need to have a subject such as a person or an animal. Instead, colors could make the painting interesting. He also believed that art and music went hand in hand. Gradually, Kandinsky began painting in a way never before seen. Soon, he was being called the founder of a new type of art known as abstract expressionism.

Kandinsky painted one of his most famous paintings in 1913. It was called *Color Study with Squares and Concentric Circles*. This painting consists of twelve circles that are inside twelve squares. Inside each circle is another circle. This is what makes the circles "concentric." None of the circles are the same size or color. They all have an individual shape and form.

The painting is made up of bright colors and shapes. Much of Kandinsky's inspiration for this painting came from classical musicians such as Mozart and Braun. To Kandinsky, certain colors represented sound. For example, the color yellow reminded him of a trumpet. The soft blue colors reminded him of the sounds of the heavens. Other colors, when painted next to one another, reminded him of chords played on a piano.

Kandinsky believed that bright colors and darker tones represent different feelings and emotions. There are reds, golds, yellows, blues, and dark greens in the painting, each color overlapping another. The softer colors such as blue and green represent calmness, while the reds and golds represent excitement. For Kandinsky, every line and shape also had meaning. Squares were peaceful; circles were spiritual; triangles were aggressive.

Next time you are in a modern art museum, see if you can find one of Kandinsky's paintings. Think about how the colors make you feel and ask yourself if they remind you of music.

Read each statement. Write *true* or *false*.

1. Abstract art is the idea that every painting needs a subject. _____

2. Kandinsky was born in Germany. _____

3. As a child, Kandinsky played the cello. _____

4. Kandinsky believed that colors alone could make a painting interesting. _____

5. Kandinsky was known as the founder of abstract expressionism. _____

6. *Color Study with Squares and Concentric Circles* has ten circles. _____

7. All of the circles in *Color Study with Squares and Concentric Circles* are exactly the same size and color. _____

8. Much of Kandinsky's inspiration for the painting came from the music of Mozart and Braun. _____

9. The color yellow reminded Kandinsky of a piano. _____

10. Kandinsky felt that there was no emotional connection to color. _____

11. Kandinsky felt that squares were peaceful shapes. _____

12. Lines had no meaning in Kandinsky's paintings. _____

Bully Prevention

A person who is being bullied might feel alone and scared. It may be difficult to attend school or other activities because focusing on subjects is hard. Bullying can involve taunting, excluding someone, or physical violence.

Bullying is a serious matter because it can have a lifelong affect. A person who has been bullied may not feel comfortable being around other people. He or she may also struggle with low self-esteem.

People become bullies for different reasons. Sometimes a bully may be bullied by someone else or could be having problems at home. Being a bully might be a way to try to become popular or to look tough in front of friends. Sometimes a bully may be secretly jealous of the person he or she is being mean to.

The best way to prevent bullying is for everyone to respect one another. This means understanding that all people are different and have their own way of doing things. It also means that a person should stop and think before saying something mean or hurtful to someone else.

If someone is bullying you, it is best to ignore the bully when possible. You can pretend you didn't hear him or her or walk away. Try not to get upset because the bully is hoping to get a reaction out of you. You may also try to respond with a joke. This may lighten the situation. If you don't want to engage with the bully, that's okay. Don't take anything a bully says personally. It's important to remember that you are not the one with the problem; the bully is. If your feelings are hurt, you can speak to an adult you trust. Actually, this is the most important thing you can do to help prevent the bullying from continuing. Your teachers, principal, and parents can help you figure out ways to make sure the bullying stops.

If you are being bullied, try not to think about revenge. This won't solve the problem and it might get you in trouble. Instead, focus on ways to prevent being bullied in the future. Make sure to keep a group of friends around you when possible. Consider changing your route to school or sitting closer to the bus driver. Walk with confidence, keeping your head up and your back straight. Most of all, remember, no one has the right to bully you. Every person deserves respect and compassion.

Answer the questions.

1. How might a person being bullied feel?

_____

2. Why might it be difficult for someone to attend school?

_____

3. What might a person who is being bullied struggle with?

_____

4. What is the best way to prevent bullying?

_____

5. What should a person do before saying something mean?

_____

6. What is a good way to lighten the situation?

_____

7. If your feelings are hurt, whom should you speak to?

_____

8. Who are three people who can help you figure out ways to stop the bullying from continuing?

_____

9. If you are being bullied, is it a good idea to think about revenge?

_____

10. Who should you surround yourself with when possible?

_____

11. If someone is bullying you on a bus, where should you sit?

_____

12. How should you walk to let people know you are not afraid?

_____

The Pull of Gravity

Imagine if you kicked a ball and it flew away instead of landing on the ground. That's what would happen without gravity. The first person to describe gravity was a scientist named Sir Isaac Newton. He wrote a book called *Mathematical Principles of Natural Philosophy* in 1687. In his book, Newton explained that gravity is the force, or pull, between two objects. Every object has gravity.

Gravity works the same on all objects. A century before Newton wrote his book, astronomer Galileo Galilei did an experiment. According to legend, he climbed the Leaning Tower of Pisa and dropped two balls of different weights. He was trying to see if one ball would fall faster than the other. He proved that it didn't matter how much the balls weighed; both balls fell at the same speed.

Not only do objects have gravity, but planets also do. Gravity from the sun keeps Earth in orbit. Without the sun's gravity, Earth would float away! Earth's gravity keeps everything close to the planet. Animals, buildings, the air we breathe, and even we humans are held here by the pull of gravity. We can't feel gravity in our bodies, but we can feel the effects of it when we jump or fall.

The amount of gravity an object or planet has depends on its size. Bigger objects have more mass and, therefore, more gravity. Like magnets, the closer an object is to another object, the stronger the gravitational pull. This is why the moon has a stronger pull on Earth than a planet like Mars. We can see examples of the moon's gravitational pull if we study tides. The moon pulls ocean water, causing the tides to rise and fall.

The weight of an object is defined by the force of gravity pulling on that object. Mass is what an object is made of. The weight can be determined by the gravity pulling on the mass. If you travel to another planet, your mass will stay the same, but your weight can change. This is because your weight depends on the gravitational pull of that particular planet. So, if you weigh 75 pounds (74 kg) on Earth, you would weigh only 28 pounds (13 kg) on Mars, but you would weigh 177 pounds (80 kg) on Jupiter.

We may not think much about gravity, but we could not live without it.

Read each question and circle the correct answer.

1. Who was the first person to describe gravity?

   a) Galileo Galilei   b) Sir Isaac Newton   c) Albert Einstein

2. What was the name of Newton's book?

   a) *Mathematical Principles of Natural Philosophy*   b) *Galileo's Law of the Pisa*
   c) *Newton's Theory of Everything*

3. What is gravity?

   a) the force, or pull, between two objects   b) how fast an object falls
   c) the cycle of day and night

4. What was Galileo's experiment?

   a) to drop two balls of the same weight   b) to drop two balls of different weight
   c) to drop two balls of the same weight but of different sizes

5. What does gravity from the sun do?

   a) keeps other solar systems in orbit   b) keeps Earth in orbit
   c) keeps the stars from floating away

6. What does the amount of gravity an object has depend on?

   a) its color   b) its shape   c) its size

7. Without the sun's gravity, what would happen to Earth?

   a) It would float away.   b) It would not be affected.
   c) It would stop spinning.

8. What do bigger objects have more of?

   a) weight   b) depth   c) mass

9. The closer an object is to another object the stronger its _____?

   a) gravitational pull   b) magnet   c) mass

10. What can we study if we want to see the moon's gravitational pull?

   a) mountains   b) sunsets   c) tides

11. What can weight be determined by?

   a) the pull of the ocean tides   b) gravity pulling on mass
   c) the size of an object

12. If you travel to another planet, what might change?

   a) your weight   b) your mass   c) your height

Celebrating Christmas

For more than 2,000 years, Christians around the world have been celebrating Christmas each year on December 25. This is a holiday that honors the birth of Jesus of Nazareth. He was a spiritual leader whose teachings are the basis of the Christian religion.

Throughout history, the middle of winter has always been a time of celebration. Even before Jesus was born, most people enjoyed festive celebrations during the winter months. This was a way to bring light and hope to the darkest time of year.

In the fourth century, Pope Julius I of Rome decided that the Church would begin celebrating the birth of Jesus. No one was sure exactly when Jesus was born, so the pope picked December 25 as the day of celebration. At first, the holiday was called the Feast of Nativity. This holiday quickly caught on. Eventually, the idea of Christmas spread to other parts of the world. However, not everybody chose to celebrate on December 25. The Greek and Russian Orthodox churches celebrate Christmas thirteen days after December 25. This is because they follow a different calendar.

The days leading up to Christmas are very busy. People spend time cooking, baking, shopping, and decorating. People put up Christmas trees in their houses and decorate them with special ornaments and lights. On Christmas morning, children wake up to see the gifts Santa Claus has left them. Santa Claus is considered the Father of Christmas.

On Christmas day, schools are closed and most people take time off from work. Some people attend church. Then they spend the day visiting with friends and family. Usually a big meal is eaten. Some people choose to eat seafood on Christmas, while others might eat ham, turkey, or another favorite dish. Many people also exchange gifts on this day.

In 1870, Christmas was declared a federal holiday. Today, Christmas is one of the most celebrated holidays in America. More than 35 million Christmas trees are sold in the United States each year. Many books, movies, and plays are about Christmas. Department stores stay open late for people to buy last-minute gifts.

Each year a few weeks before Christmas, a giant tree is brought to Rockefeller Center in New York City. Here, tens of thousands of people crowd around and listen to entertainment while watching the famous tree-lighting ceremony.

Write a synonym for each underlined word or phrase. Use the words from the word bank.

celebration	honors	holiday	exchange	ornaments	attend
spread	busy	choose	declared	buy	considered

1. Christmas is a holiday that <u>pays tribute</u> to the birth of Jesus of Nazareth. _____

2. Throughout history, the middle of winter has always been a time for <u>festivities</u>. _____

3. At first, the Christmas <u>observance</u> was called the Feast of Nativity. _____

4. The idea of Christmas <u>extended</u> to other parts of the world. _____

5. The days leading up to Christmas are <u>full of activity</u> with cooking, baking, shopping, and decorating. _____

6. People put up Christmas trees in their houses and decorate them with special <u>trinkets</u> and lights. _____

7. Some people <u>go to</u> church on Christmas Day. _____

8. Some people <u>decide</u> to eat seafood on Christmas, while others might eat another favorite dish. _____

9. Santa is <u>thought to be</u> the Father of Christmas. _____

10. Many people <u>swap</u> gifts on Christmas. _____

11. In 1870, Christmas was <u>confirmed</u> a federal holiday. _____

12. Department stores stay open late on Christmas for people to <u>purchase</u> last-minute gifts. _____

Let's Make Hummus

Chickpeas are a type of bean that was first found in West Asia. They are filled with protein and fiber, which means that they are healthy for you. It also means that when you eat them, you stay full longer.

People began farming chickpeas as early as 10,000 BCE in places like Turkey. In ancient times, these beans were a good source of food because they could be dried and stored through the winter months. One way to prepare chickpeas was to boil them and then add them to stew. They could also be mixed with vegetables or roasted over fire. Sometimes people boiled the beans and mashed them up with other ingredients such as garlic and olive oil to make hummus. This simple dish quickly became a popular food throughout West Asia and parts of Africa, including Egypt. Today, many people around the world still enjoy this easy-to-make recipe. Are you ready to try it?

You will need:

❑ Can opener ❑ Colander ❑ Small, sharp knife ❑ Measuring cups
❑ Blender ❑ Spatula ❑ Small bowl

Ingredients:

3 cans of chickpeas $1/4$ teaspoon pepper 2 large cloves of garlic
1 large fresh lemon $1/2$ teaspoon salt
$1/4$ cup olive oil $1/2$ cup water

Step 1: Wash your hands before you begin.

Step 2: Line up all the ingredients on a counter or table.

Step 3: Carefully open the cans of chickpeas and pour them into the colander to drain away the liquid.

Step 4: Rinse the chickpeas under cold running water.

Step 5: Carefully peel the skins off the garlic cloves.

Step 6: With an adult's supervision, cut the lemon in half and then squeeze all the juice into a measuring cup until you have $1/4$ cup.

Step 7: With an adult's supervision, put all the ingredients in the blender except for the water.

Step 8: Make sure the blender lid is closed tightly and then purée the ingredients until creamy.

Step 9: Turn the blender to the off position and taste your hummus. If it is too dry, add some of the water and blend again. Keep adding water and blending as needed.

Step 10: Using your spatula, scoop the hummus into the small bowl.

Step 11: Drizzle a teaspoon of olive oil on top.

Step 12: Get your favorite veggies, pita, or crackers and start dipping!

What's the order? Number the steps *1* to *12*.

1. _____ Drizzle a teaspoon of olive oil on top.

2. _____ Turn the blender to the off position and taste your hummus. If it is too dry, add some of the water and blend again. Keep adding water and blending as needed.

3. _____ Carefully peel the skins off the garlic cloves.

4. _____ Get your favorite veggies, pita, or crackers and start dipping!

5. _____ Wash your hands before you begin.

6. _____ Make sure the blender lid is closed tightly and then purée the ingredients until creamy.

7. _____ Line up all the ingredients on a counter or table.

8. _____ With an adult's supervision, cut the lemon in half and then squeeze all the juice into a measuring cup until you have $1/4$ cup.

9. _____ Rinse the chickpeas under cold running water.

10. _____ With an adult's supervision, put all the ingredients in the blender except for the water.

11. _____ Carefully open the cans of chickpeas and pour them into the colander to drain away the liquid.

12. _____ Using your spatula, scoop the hummus into a small bowl.

A Time of Rebirth

The Renaissance was a time in history when the people of Europe became more interested in the world around them. Beginning in the early fourteenth century, artists began creating vibrant artwork, new inventions made life easier, and explorers navigated unchartered lands.

The years leading up to the fourteenth century were known as the Middle Ages. During this time, life was hard. Most people in Europe were very poor and illiterate, meaning they couldn't read. Many countries were constantly at war. These conditions began to cost people their health and even life.

Around this time a group of scholars in Florence, Italy, came together to study the cultures of ancient Rome and Greece. They realized that in ancient times, literature and art flourished. The scholars wanted to go back to those ideas. They decided to form a group called the Humanists. Humanists felt it was important to enjoy life. They knew this could be accomplished by bringing art, music, and science back to their society. Soon the Middle Ages were viewed as the Dark Ages. Humanists brought light back to daily life. This is why this period is called the Renaissance. The word *Renaissance* means "rebirth."

Over time, these new ideas began spreading from northern Italy to other Italian cities such as Naples and Venice. Soon, these "reborn" areas became major ports for trade with the Middle East.

Trade made many families wealthy. These families began buying paintings and sculptures. They also began building beautiful architecture.

One of the first Renaissance painters was Giotto di Bondone. His work was different from the art of the Middle Ages because he painted his subjects as they actually looked. Paintings before this time didn't look very realistic. Also, now paintings focused more on nature and less on religion.

When the printing press was invented in 1450, it had a huge impact on daily life. Before this time, every book had to be written by hand. That meant few copies were made and most people never had a chance to read. The printing press changed all that. A goldsmith named Johannes Gutenberg had come up with an idea of creating moveable type that could be painted with ink and then pressed onto paper. Many copies of each page could be made, and the pages could be bound into books.

Explorers also began sailing to far-off lands. In 1492, Christopher Columbus discovered the Americas for Spain.

With these discoveries, inventions, and art, new ideas quickly spread throughout all of Europe. The light had been brought back, and people were no longer living in dark times.

Read each statement. Write *true* or *false*.

1. The Renaissance was a time of great change. _____

2. The years leading up to the Renaissance were
a time of new discoveries. _____

3. The word *illiterate* refers to people who can't read. _____

4. There were many wars during the Middle Ages. _____

5. The Renaissance began in Florence, Italy. _____

6. Scholars came together to study ancient Egypt. _____

7. These scholars believed that in ancient times literature
and art were meaningless. _____

8. The scholars of the Renaissance became known as Humanists. _____

9. The word *Renaissance* means "rebirth." _____

10. Trade with other countries failed to bring money to Italy. _____

11. Renaissance paintings were more realistic than
those from the Middle Ages. _____

12. The printing press had little effect on the number of
people who could read books. _____

Learning About the Islamic Faith

With more than 1.5 billion followers, Islam is the second-largest religion on the planet. The people who follow the Islamic religion are called Muslims. Though Muslims live in countries throughout the world, the largest population with this faith can be found in Indonesia and Pakistan.

The word *Islam* means "submission," or "surrender." Muslims feel that they can find a path to peace by submitting, or surrendering, to the will of Allah. *Allah* is the Muslim name for God. Muslims believe in only one God and follow the teachings of Muhammad, a prophet who was born in Saudi Arabia in 570 CE. Muhammad was a shepherd and a merchant who felt that people had strayed from their religious and moral beliefs. He spent a lot of time praying and meditating in the mountains. After a while, he believed that he began receiving messages from Allah through the angel Gabriel. He then preached to others what he had learned. He told his followers that there was no other God but Allah and that people should lead an honorable life. These teachings were recorded in the Muslim holy book called the Qur'an. The Qur'an is considered the word of God as told to Mohammad.

The main teachings of Islam are based on what is known as the Five Pillars. This is a guide to remind Muslims how best to lead their daily life and put their beliefs into practice. The first one is *Shahadah*. This is when Muslims declare their belief in Allah and the teachings of Mohammad. *Salat* is the ritual prayer. Muslims pray five times a day: dawn, noon, mid-afternoon, sunset, and night. When Muslims pray, they often do so in a mosque, or temple. If they aren't close to a mosque, they can pray almost anywhere. No matter where they are, they turn to pray facing the holy city of Mecca in Saudi Arabia. *Zakat* is the belief that one must donate part of his or her salary to the poor. *Sawm* is the word for fasting, or going without food for a time. During the month called Ramadan, Muslims fast during the day. They do this to remind themselves of what they have and to show equality with people who are not as fortunate as they are. Finally, the fifth pillar is *Hajj*. This word means "pilgrimage." All Muslims believe that it is important to take a pilgrimage to visit the holy city of Mecca at least once in their life.

Draw a line to match each description to the correct term.

1. This word means "submission" or "surrender."

2. Islam has this many followers.

3. The largest population of Muslims
   can be found in Indonesia and here.

4. Muslims follow the teachings of this prophet.

5. Mohammad spent a lot of time doing this in the mountains.

6. The name of the angel who came to Mohammad.

7. The kind of life Mohammad preached that people should live.

8. The name for the Muslim holy book.

9. The main teachings of Islam are based on this.

10. The amount of times each day that Muslims pray.

11. The place Muslims go to pray.

12. The holy city where Muslims go for their pilgrimage.

a) 1.5 billion

b) Mecca

c) Mohammad

d) Qur'an

e) five

f) honorable

g) Pakistan

h) Islam

i) Five Pillars

j) Gabriel

k) praying

l) mosque

The First Lady of the World

Eleanor Roosevelt was born on October 11, 1884, in New York City. She grew up surrounded by wealth but had a difficult childhood. In 1892, when she was eight years old, her mother died. Two years later, in 1894, her father died, too. Roosevelt was an orphan. She lived with her grandmother in upstate New York. When she turned eighteen, she headed back to New York City to teach.

In 1905, Eleanor married her fifth cousin Franklin Delano Roosevelt. Her uncle Theodore Roosevelt, the president of the United States, walked her down the aisle at her wedding. Together, the Roosevelts had six children.

When World War I broke out in 1914, Eleanor Roosevelt joined the Red Cross and volunteered to work in hospitals to help wounded soldiers. She also became very active in helping her husband pursue his political career. In 1921, Franklin contracted a disease called polio. This left him unable to walk. Eleanor cared for Franklin and continued to help further his political goals. In 1933, Franklin Delano Roosevelt became the thirty-second president of the United States.

As first lady, Roosevelt traveled around the country to see firsthand the living and working conditions of the people. This was during the Great Depression, when many people were unemployed and struggling. She would then report her findings back to her husband. Eleanor became known as the president's eyes and ears and was often called the First Lady of the World. In 1935, she began writing a column about her adventures around the country. She was an activist for poor and disadvantaged people and hoped to help them by giving them a voice.

Franklin Roosevelt died during his presidency on April 12, 1945. This didn't stop Eleanor Roosevelt from continuing to serve the people of her country. President Truman appointed her to chair the Human Rights Commission for the United Nations. She worked very hard and drafted a document called the Universal Declaration of Human Rights. This was a declaration explaining the basic rights of all humans. It was adopted by the United Nations in 1948. She resigned from her position in 1953 but continued to work on humanitarian causes. She also continued to speak publically, write books, and give lectures.

Roosevelt died on November 7, 1962. She is buried alongside her husband. People who are interested in learning more about the Roosevelts can visit their estate in Hyde Park, New York.

Complete the timeline with the correct dates.

1. _____ Eleanor Roosevelt was born in New York City.

2. _____ Eleanor's mother died.

3. _____ Eleanor's father died.

4. _____ Eleanor married Franklin Delano Roosevelt.

5. _____ World War I broke out.

6. _____ Franklin contracted polio.

7. _____ Franklin Delano Roosevelt became the thirty-second president of the United States.

8. _____ Eleanor began writing a column about her adventures around the country.

9. _____ Franklin died during his presidency.

10. _____ The United Nations adopted the Universal Declaration of Human Rights.

11. _____ Eleanor resigned from her position as chair of the Human Rights Commission.

12. _____ Eleanor died.

Stressed Out

Have you ever had a bellyache before a big event? Maybe you've had trouble sleeping because you were worried about a test you were taking the next day. These are all signs of stress. Stress is a feeling in your body you get when you are anxious about something. Stress can cause you to feel worried, frustrated, angry, or even scared. Everybody gets stressed out sometimes!

Not all stress is bad for you. There are good stresses and bad stresses. Good stress might happen when you have to do a presentation for your school science fair. Just thinking about it might give you butterflies in your stomach. But good stress can help you accomplish tasks. You might be nervous about your presentation so you study harder and prepare for it. Bad stress happens over time. If your friends are always fighting or if you're having trouble at school that is bad stress. Bad stress doesn't help you, and sometimes it can actually make you physically sick.

Luckily, there are ways to manage stress so it doesn't become too overwhelming. Talking about your feelings is often helpful. Discussing your problems with an adult you trust, such as a parent or a teacher, can make you feel better. They may be able to give you advice or help you come up with a solution.

Another way to manage stress is to make a list of what you have going on in your life. It could be that you have too many activities planned and not enough time to relax. Even if these activities are fun, they may cause stress and make you tired. You might consider cutting back on some of your after-school plans.

Other ways to handle stress are to make sure you are getting enough sleep, eating healthy foods, and exercising. If you are sleepy because you've stayed up too late, your body will have less tolerance for the demands you face each day. Healthy food helps support your body throughout the day. If you are eating foods that are high in sugar, your brain has to work harder to stay focused. Exercise helps you burn off energy and gets your blood circulating.

You can also do breathing exercises. Take a deep breath in through your nose and exhale through your mouth. This is a great exercise to do because you can do it anytime or anywhere.

If you take care of yourself, get enough exercise, make time to relax, and, most important, have fun, you will likely be less stressed!

Use words from the word bank to complete each sentence.

Everybody	sick	presentation	feeling	time	tasks
problems	after-school	list	sleep	sugar	Exercise

1. Stress is a _____ in your body you get when you are anxious about something.

2. _____ gets stressed out.

3. Good stress can happen when you have to do a _____ for a science fair at school.

4. Good stress helps you accomplish _____.

5. Bad stress happens over _____.

6. Bad stress can make you _____.

7. Discussing your _____ with an adult can make you feel better.

8. One way to manage stress is to make a _____ about what is going on in your life.

9. You might consider cutting back on some of your _____ plans.

10. Other ways to help with stress are to make sure you get enough _____, eat healthy foods, and exercise.

11. If you eat foods high in _____, your brain has to work harder to stay focused.

12. _____ helps you burn energy and gets your blood circulating.

Understanding Minerals

Have you ever looked at a mineral and wondered how it was made or where it came from? Minerals are solid inorganic substances. This means they are not made of liquid or gas and do not come from living matter such as plants or animals. Humans cannot make minerals because they are naturally occurring in nature.

Minerals are made up of a mixture of chemical elements. They also have an ordered atomic arrangement. This means the chemical elements are arranged in a specific way. Most minerals come in interesting shapes, sizes, and colors that are fun to look at. Scientists have come up with a system to identify a mineral's physical characteristics.

Cleavage is the term used to describe how a mineral breaks into pieces. Minerals can break in angles that form planes. Depending on how these planes break, a mineral can form various shapes such as cubes or diamonds. One mineral that often breaks this way is called mica.

Fracture is when a mineral breaks into a shape other than a flat plan. The mineral can be smooth, uneven, or splintery, or have rough edges.

Hardness is another way a mineral's physical characteristics can be identified. This depends on how easy it is to scratch the surface of the mineral. Mineralogists use the Mohs Scale of Hardness to test how hard a mineral is. This scale is based on a number system from one to ten. Minerals like talc are easy to scratch so they rank number one. Diamonds are the hardest at number ten.

Luster describes how a mineral looks when it reflects light. Mineralogists define luster in two ways: metallic and nonmetallic. Metallic minerals, such as hematite, are shiny. Nonmetallic minerals can look silky, can be clear like a diamond, or can look like glass. Some—like the mineral graphite—even look greasy.

Specific gravity measures how heavy a mineral is compared to how heavy water is. A scale called a Jolly Balance is used to determine this. First the mineral is weighed in the air. Then it is weighed in water. Last, an equation is applied to get the specific gravity.

Streak is the color of powder left behind when a mineral is scraped across a glass plate. Hard minerals will not leave a streak. Instead they might scratch the plate. The color of the streak can help identify the mineral.

Next time you find some minerals, see if you can identify any of their characteristics.

Read the entries in the first column. Check off which physical characteristic each is referring to.

	Cleavage	Fracture	Hardness	Luster	Streak	Specific Gravity
1. The color of powder left behind when a mineral is scraped across a glass plate						
2. Measures how heavy a mineral is compared to how much it weighs in water						
3. Minerals can form shapes such as cubes or diamonds when they break this way.						
4. Can be defined as metallic or nonmetallic						
5. The Mohs Scale of Hardness determines this.						
6. When a mineral breaks like this it can have rough edges.						
7. A Jolly Balance is used to measure this.						
8. Describes how a mineral looks when it reflects light						
9. Depends on how easy it is to scratch the surface of the mineral						
10. When a mineral breaks into a shape other than a flat plane						
11. A hard mineral will not leave this.						
12. The term that describes when a mineral breaks into planes						

The Cradle of Civilization

Ancient Mesopotamia is known as the "cradle of civilization." This is because the very first towns and cities grew in this area in approximately 5000 BCE. Mesopotamia was located in what we now call southern Iraq. A people known as Sumerians first began settling here because the land was fertile and easy to farm.

Over time, towns and cities began to grow and governments formed to make laws. This growth also led to a division of class systems. The head of the Sumerian society was the king. Next came the priests. The priests were not only the center of religious life, but they were also doctors. Wealthy people made up the rest of the upper class.

Besides farming in the countryside, there were many new opportunities for jobs as the towns grew. The middle class was made up of craftsman, merchants, and government workers. As the first people to have a written language, scribes became necessary to write down information. Laborers and farmers made up the lower class. The Sumerians also kept slaves who were at the bottom of the class system. They had no rights and were owned by the wealthy. Slaves were usually prisoners who had been taken captive during battles.

In ancient Mesopotamia, homes were simple. They were rectangular houses made of mud bricks. This type of material insulated the houses, keeping them warm in the winter and cool in the summer. During warmer weather, it was common for people to sleep outside on top of their flat roofs.

Clothing in ancient Mesopotamia was made from sheepskin or wool. Both men and women wore skirts, but a woman's skirt was longer. Women also wore jewelry, especially rings, and kept their hair long. Both men and women decorated their faces with makeup.

People often gathered together for festivals to play music on instruments such as the drum, flute, or harp. They also had storytellers who passed stories down through the generations, either verbally or by writing them on tablets. Wealthy people also enjoyed art and poetry, which was mainly based on religious beliefs.

Much of daily life was centered around religion. The Sumerians worshipped various gods and goddesses, believing that the gods had the power to influence their fate. Every city had a large temple in which priests made sacrifices.

Daily life in ancient Mesopotamia meant working hard, spending time with family, and engaging in religious worship and community gatherings.

Answer the questions.

1. What is ancient Mesopotamia known as?

_____

2. What do we now call the part of the world where ancient Mesopotamia was located?

_____

3. Why did Sumerians first begin to settle this area?

_____

4. Why was it necessary for the Sumerians to have scribes?

_____

5. Who was the head of Sumerian society?

_____

6. Besides being at the center of religious life, what else did priests do?

_____

7. Who made up the lower class?

_____

8. When did Sumerians capture slaves?

_____

9. What were houses in Mesopotamia made from?

_____

10. Where did Sumerians sometimes sleep when it was hot outside?

_____

11. What did people use to make clothing?

_____

12. What were some of the instruments used during festive occasions?

_____

Confucianism

Confucianism is a philosophy or idea about how people should live. Some people consider Confucianism a religion, while others believe it is more of a way of life.

In 551 BCE, Kung Fu-Tzu was born into a poor family in the province of Lu, China. The western translation of Kung Fu-Tzu's name is Confucius. As Confucius grew, he saw that society had many problems. He knew that he wanted to spend his life helping to make the world a better place. When Confucius was old enough, he began looking for a job with the Chinese government. He felt that getting a good position in government would allow him to make changes that might help people learn how to lead better lives. Though he continued to believe in a strong government, he soon realized that he would be more helpful to people if he became a teacher. With this idea in mind, Confucius became the first teacher in China who thought that education was important for everybody. Before that, only the wealthy hired private tutors to learn. Confucius felt that all human beings should be taught ways to improve their lives.

Confucius came up with five ethics, or qualities, to live by. They are kindness, righteousness, sobriety, wisdom, and trustworthiness. He believed that it was important to be loyal and think about the needs of others. He also outlined ways for people to live in peace and harmony. One of the best ways to do this was to treat others with kindness. He explained that if you are kind to others, they will be kind to you and your life will be better.

Confucius felt that it was very important for children to respect their parents and elders. Another idea he believed in was to avoid becoming too angry or emotional. Over time, more and more people began to follow Confucius's teachings. He did not write down his ideas, but his followers did. There are five texts that include poetry, history, rituals, and sayings.

During his lifetime, Confucius did not have too many followers. However, after he died, in 479 BCE, people continued to put his beliefs into practice. They even built temples in his honor. A hundred years later, the emperor of China began using Confucius's ideas to help him rule his people. This made Confucianism more popular.

Today, more than five million people practice the ideas of Confucianism. Mostly these people live in China. Some of them practice other religions, but they still consider themselves Confucians.

Read each question and circle the correct answer.

1. Where was Confucius born?

   a) China   b) Japan   c) India

2. When Confucius was growing up, what did he notice?

   a) that people had too much money   b) that society had problems
   c) that there wasn't enough time to rest

3. What did Confucius want to spend his life doing?

   a) studying   b) making the world a better place   c) learning to cook

4. When he was old enough, where did Confucius first try to find a job?

   a) in government   b) as a scribe   c) as a doctor

5. After working in the government, what did Confucius then decide to do?

   a) retire   b) nothing   c) teach

6. Before Confucius became a teacher, what did most wealthy people do?

   a) hired tutors   b) studied in other countries   c) didn't learn

7. Who did Confucius believe should be educated?

   a) elderly people   b) young children   c) everybody

8. What did Confucius believe would happen to people who were kind to others?

   a) Others would be kind to them.   b) Nothing would happen.
   c) People would still be mean.

9. Who wrote down Confucius's ideas?

   a) he did   b) his followers   c) the emperor

10. What did Confucius's followers build in his honor?

    a) houses   b) gardens   c) temples

11. What did Confucius's teachings say that children should do?

    a) respect their parents   b) play all the time   c) whatever they want

12. How many followers of Confucianism are there today?

    a) one million   b) none   c) more than five million

Let's Play Field Hockey!

Field hockey is a sport played on a large grassy field. It is a lot like soccer in that the object of the game is to get the ball past the goalie. Only, instead of using a soccer ball, players use curved wooden sticks and a small, plastic ball. This game has been around in different forms for a long time. Ancient Greeks, Arabs, and Romans all had their own unique versions. In the nineteenth century, field hockey became popular in England. India made field hockey its national game in 1928. Today, people around the world continue to enjoy it.

Field hockey is played on a field that is 100 yards (91.4 m) long and 60 yards (54.9 m) wide. There is one centerline and two 25-yard (22.9-m) lines. There are eleven players on each team. In order to score, a player must shoot the ball into the goal. Are you ready to learn the basics?

Step 1: Get your gear! You'll need a field hockey stick that is right for your weight and size. You'll also need cleats, shin guards, goggles, and a mouth guard.

Step 2: Gather your friends and choose teams.

Step 3: Warm up for the game by running around the field and stretching.

Step 4: Grip your hockey stick. Using your left hand, hold your stick at the top with your thumb pointing down toward the hooked end of the stick. Place your right hand on the stick at a lower point.

Step 5: Practice guiding the stick with your left hand. Use your right hand to support it.

Step 6: Practice your stance. Keep your head and chest up while bending at the waist. Point your left foot in front of you, while keeping your right foot back for support.

Step 7: Keep your knees bent and aim for the ball.

Step 8: As the ball comes toward you, step back so it has a chance to slow down before you try to stop it. Lean the stick in the direction of your body and try to make contact with the ball.

Step 9: Always use the flat side of the stick when you hit the ball. You can dribble the ball with small taps to move it forward. This allows you to keep the ball in your possession.

Step 10: When you are ready, hit the ball. As you become more advanced, you will learn different types of shots.

Step 11: Try to aim for the goal.

Step 12: Keep practicing. Field hockey is a hard game to learn, but it can be a lot of fun.

What's the order? Number the events *1* to *12*.

1. _____ Try to aim for the goal.

2. _____ As the ball comes toward you, step back so it has a chance to slow down before you try to stop it. Lean the stick in the direction of your body and try to make contact with the ball.

3. _____ Keep practicing. Field hockey is a hard game to learn, but it can be a lot of fun.

4. _____ Practice your stance. Keep your head and chest up while bending at the waist. Point your left foot in front of you, while keeping your right foot back for support.

5. _____ When you are ready, hit the ball. As you become more advanced, you will learn different types of shots.

6. _____ Gather your friends and choose teams.

7. _____ Grip your hockey stick. Using your left hand, hold your stick at the top with your thumb pointing down toward the hooked end of the stick. Place your right hand on the stick at a lower point.

8. _____ Get your gear! You'll need a field hockey stick that is right for your weight and size. You'll also need cleats, shin guards, goggles, and a mouth guard.

9. _____ Practice guiding the stick with your left hand. Use your right hand to support it.

10. _____ Keep your knees bent and aim for the ball.

11. _____ Warm up for the game by running around the field and stretching.

12. _____ Always use the flat side of the stick when you hit the ball. You can dribble the ball with small taps to move it forward. This allows you to keep the ball in your possession.

Ocean Currents and Our Climate

Do you like riding waves in the ocean? Have you ever wondered where these waves come from and how they influence our planet? Ocean currents cause the waves. When talking about the ocean, the word *currents* describes the movement of water.

There are different types of currents. Surface currents are caused by wind and occur near the surface of the ocean. As wind blows over the ocean, it pushes the currents. When the wind changes, so do the surface currents. One well-known surface current is the Gulf Stream. Trade winds in the Atlantic Ocean move the currents in a northwesterly direction. The Gulf Stream moves north along the east coast of the United States from the Gulf of Mexico to Canada. It travels at about 4 miles per hour (6.4 kph) and transports more water than all the rivers in the world combined.

Tidal currents form from the gravitational pull of the sun and moon. The gravitational force of the moon pulls the ocean, causing the water to bulge. These currents are based on the cycle of the moon and can be either very strong and fast or very slow and weak. Tidal currents can move sediment over long distances, changing Earth's landscape.

Deep-water currents move slowly and can be found hundreds of feet below the surface of the ocean. These currents can form based on the salinity, or saltiness, of the ocean, the density of the ocean, and the temperature. Currents in the Northern Hemisphere flow clockwise. In the Southern Hemisphere, they flow counterclockwise.

Ocean currents have a huge effect on climate and life forms around the world. The ocean absorbs solar heat from the atmosphere. This means that as the planet gets warmer, the ocean gets warmer, too. This can have a negative effect on fish and other sea creatures. They must adapt to the warmer temperatures, swim to cooler waters, or die.

Another example of how the currents affect climate change can be seen in Europe. The Atlantic Ocean currents carry warm water northward along the west coast of Europe. The colder water in the north sinks deeper into the ocean, and the warm water stays on the surface. As the warm water cools, it sinks down to where the colder water is. This water travels south, warms up in the warmer climates, and rises to the surface again. Then it travels back to the northern oceans again. The action is like a huge conveyer belt moving in a slow circle. Scientists even named it the Great Ocean Conveyor Belt! The warm water that has traveled north heats the air above the ocean. This makes places like Great Britain hotter than they should be and causes climate changes.

Circle the correct word to complete each sentence.

1. When talking about the ocean, the word *currents* describes the movement of _____ (water/sediment).

2. Wind causes _____ (deep water/surface) currents.

3. When wind blows across the ocean, it _____ (pulls/pushes) surface currents.

4. The Gulf Stream travels north from the Gulf of Mexico to _____ (Canada/Greenland).

5. _____ (Tidal/Deep water) currents form from the gravitational pull of the sun and the moon.

6. Tidal currents are based on the cycle of the _____ (wind/moon).

7. Tidal currents move _____ (wind/sediment) over long distances.

8. _____ (Deep water/Surface) currents are found hundreds of feet below the surface of the ocean.

9. Deep water currents can form based on the _____ (saltiness/color) of the ocean.

10. The ocean absorbs _____ (sand/heat) from the atmosphere.

11. The Great Ocean Conveyer Belt brings _____ (cold/warm) water into colder regions.

12. Heat being stored in the ocean is partly responsible for _____ (population/climate) change.

Understanding Free Enterprise

Do you ever think about what it would be like to run a business? In the United States, people can choose the type of business they want to have. This is called free enterprise.

Free enterprise is the idea that a person has the right to start a business for profit. It also means that the person who owns the business gets to decide what kind of fees to charge, what to sell, and how many hours to work. The government has laws to make sure that business owners do not cheat others. As long as business owners follow these laws, there are very few restrictions on how they can run their business. In a free-enterprise system, business owners can buy land, buildings, or property and open their businesses where they think they will do well.

As a consumer, being part of the free-enterprise system means you can spend your money where you want. Sometimes you may even have different businesses competing with one another to sell you the same products. Businesses may have sales or special deals to try to get you to shop at their stores. Having this choice often makes products less expensive. It can also ensure that the products you are buying are good quality. Business owners know that you can shop somewhere else, so they want to make sure you are a happy customer.

But what happens when everyone wants the same products? This is known as supply and demand. If there is already a large supply of the product on the market, the price will go down. If there is a big demand but little supply, the price goes up.

Being part of the free-enterprise system means people have the right to work where they want. In the United States, the government cannot tell anyone how to earn a living. This is not the case in other parts of the world. In some countries, the government decides what kind of jobs people have. Such governments also decide who can own a business. Then they put in place strict laws about running that business. Because of this, consumers in these countries are often limited in what they are allowed to buy. In countries that have a system of free enterprise, there are many more opportunities for people.

Read each statement. Write *true* or *false*.

1. Free enterprise is the idea that a person has the right to start a business for profit. _____

2. With free enterprise, a business owner does not get to decide what fees to charge. _____

3. With free enterprise, a business owner can choose how many hours to work. _____

4. In a free-enterprise system, the government doesn't make any laws at all. _____

5. In the United States, business owners can buy land or property and open a business where they think it will do well. _____

6. As a consumer in a free-enterprise system, you can spend your money where you want. _____

7. Businesses never compete with each other to sell the same products. _____

8. When demand for a product is high, a business owner can raise the price. _____

9. If there is a large supply of products on the market, the price goes up. _____

10. Being part of the free-enterprise system means that everyone has a right to work where they want. _____

11. In the United States, the government can tell you how to earn a living. _____

12. In some countries, consumers are limited in what they are allowed to buy. _____

The Celebration of Vaisakhi

Vaisakhi is the celebration of the Sikh New Year. It is also meant to honor the birth of Sikhism and the founding of the Sikh community. It takes place every year in April.

Before becoming the most important festival for Sikhs, Vaisakhi was celebrated as a harvest festival in Punjab, India. In 1699, during the yearly festival, a religious leader known as Guru Gobind Singh appeared from a tent to make an announcement to the people. He told anyone who was prepared to give his life in the name of religion to step forward. One young man presented himself and disappeared into a tent with the guru. Moments later, the guru came out of the tent with his sword covered in blood. Then he asked for more volunteers. One by one people began going into the tent. Each time, the guru came out with his sword covered in blood. In total, five people had gone into the tent. The people at the festival were worried. But soon, all five came out of the tent unharmed and wearing turbans on their heads.

The guru explained that this had been a test to see who had religious faith. From then on, the five people who had gone into the tent became known as the Beloved Five. The guru then performed a ceremony called *Amrit* in which he sprinkled the five men with water that had been mixed with sugar. This was done to remind them that it is important to be strong, but it is also important to have a sweet nature. They became the first members of the Khalsa, or Sihk community. That day, many others were initiated into the community. They pledged their belief in one god and their commitment to treat all people equally.

As part of the celebration of *Vaisakhi*, Sikhs worship in temples called *Gudwaras*. They decorate the temples and put up a new Sikh flag each year. The holiday is celebrated with festivals, parades, and dancing. People also sing hymns known as *kirtan* and share a special meal in a kitchen called a *langar*.

Many Sihks choose this special day to be initiated into the community of Khalsa. Once they do this, they are agreeing to follow a certain way of life. They agree to worship one god, recite prayers daily, and read religious texts. They also commit to living a truthful life and using good moral judgment.

Write an antonym for each underlined word or phrase. Use words from the word bank.

unprepared	leaving	least	weak	last	bitter
carefree	old	refusal	disagree	ordinary	bad

1. Before becoming the most important festival for Sikhs, Vaisakhi was celebrated as a harvest festival in Punjab, India.

   _____

2. The guru told anyone who was prepared to give his life in the name of religion to step forward.

   _____

3. One by one people began going into the tent.

   _____

4. The people at the festival were worried.

   _____

5. They were sprinkled with water to remind them that it is important to be strong.

   _____

6. The water was mixed with sugar to remind them to have a sweet nature.

   _____

7. These men became the first members of the *Khalsa*, or Sihk community.

   _____

8. They pledged their belief in one god and their commitment to treat all people equally.

   _____

9. They decorate the temples and put up a new Sikh flag each year.

   _____

10. People sing hymns known as *kirtan* and share a special meal called *langar*.

    _____

11. They agree to worship one god, recite prayers daily, and read religious texts.

    _____

12. They also commit to living a truthful life and using good moral judgment.

    _____

Space Objects

Have you ever looked up at the night sky and noticed a shooting star? It's an amazing sight, but did you know that they are not stars at all? They are actually meteors burning up as they enter Earth's atmosphere.

Our solar system is a mysterious place made up of many different objects. Some of them are meteoroids, asteroids, and comets.

A meteoroid is a small piece of rock that shoots through space. It can be as tiny as a particle of dust or as big as a house. Earth's gravity is responsible for pulling meteorites from space into our atmosphere. They can travel as fast as 26 miles (41.8 km) per second! Once they enter Earth's atmosphere and begin to burn, they become known as meteors. Millions of meteors fall from the sky every day. Sometimes a group of meteors may fall at the same time. This is called a meteor shower. A meteor that doesn't completely burn when it enters the atmosphere is called a meteorite. Occasionally meteorites fall to the ground, often causing damage to houses and vehicles.

Comets orbit the sun and are made up of ice, dust, and rock. As a comet moves closer to the sun, the ice begins to melt. As the ice melts, gases and plasma are left behind, leaving a fuzzy outline around the comet. This fuzzy outline is called a coma. As the comet moves through space, the coma begins to trail behind, creating a tail. There are short-period comets and long-period comets. Short-period comets orbit the sun in periods of less than two hundred years. Long-period comets orbit the sun in periods of more than two hundred years. The most famous comet is called Haley's Comet. It is a short-period comet that can be seen from Earth approximately every seventy-six years.

Asteroids are similar to comets. They are made of rock and metal but do not have a coma. They are considered minor planets called planetoids. Asteroids come in all different sizes. They can be a few feet in diameter, or they can be hundreds of miles in diameter. The asteroid belt is where most asteroids can be found. This belt orbits the sun between Mars and Jupiter. The largest asteroid is called Ceres. It is so big that it is considered a dwarf planet.

Next time you look up at the sky, think of all the truly amazing things to be found up there!

Read each question and circle the correct answer.

1. What is a shooting star?

    a) asteroid   b) comet   c) meteor

2. What is a meteoroid?

    a) a small piece of rock   b) a gas   c) a large piece of glass

3. What is responsible for pulling meteorites into our atmosphere?

    a) the moon   b) gravity   c) the sun

4. How fast can meteorites travel?

    a) 26 miles per second   b) 26 miles per hour   c) 26 miles per year

5. Once a meteorite enters Earth's atmosphere and begins to burn, what is it called?

    a) coma   b) asteroid   c) meteor

6. When many meteors fall from the sky, what is it called?

    a) meteor shower   b) meteor bath   c) meteor falls

7. What do comets orbit?

    a) Earth   b) the sun   c) the moon

8. What is the fuzzy outline around the comet called?

    a) coma   b) fuzz   c) air

9. How often do short-term comets orbit the sun?

    a) in periods of more than two hundred years
    b) in periods of less than two hundred years   c) in periods of twenty years

10. What is the name of one of the most famous comets?

    a) Mars Comet   b) Orion's Belt   c) Haley's Comet

11. How often can we see Haley's Comet from Earth?

    a) approximately every seventy-six years   b) approximately every seven years
    c) approximately every 750 years

12. Which planets do the asteroid belt orbit?

    a) Saturn and Mars   b) Mars and Jupiter   c) Jupiter and Uranus

The Valley of the Kings

The Valley of the Kings is a sacred ancient burial ground. It is located on the hot, dry, west bank of the Nile River in Egypt. Buried here are more than sixty important pharaohs, or rulers. This is a very special place where many treasures and mysteries have been uncovered.

Until 1500 BCE, most pharaohs chose to be buried in beautiful pyramids. The people of ancient Egypt believed in taking all their belongings with them to the afterlife. When the pharaohs died, the people who buried them made sure to pack their tomb with riches and other items to keep them comfortable. This included furniture, cookware, brightly colored carvings, jewels, and even preserved food.

Unfortunately, everyone knew where the pharaohs were buried. This made it easy for tomb raiders to break into their pyramids and steal everything. When it was time for King Thutmose I to build his tomb, he decided he was going to do something different. He was the first pharaoh who planned to be buried in a secret place. Tomb raiders would have difficulty finding his tomb. Legend has it that the builder of King Thutmose I's tomb captured foreigners and forced them to construct the tombs at the Valley of the Kings. Once they were done, the builder killed the foreigners. This meant that no one would find out the location of the tomb.

Some of the tombs at the Valley of the Kings are built into a mountainside. Others are buried deep under the valley floor. Each tomb has unique traits and was built in a different size. Some have long corridors, while others have many rooms or chambers. Some of the tombs were even built with trap doors to catch tomb raiders. Despite the pharaohs' best efforts, most of the tombs were raided over the centuries and all the valuables stolen. There has been one exception. In 1922, an Egyptologist named Howard Carter discovered King Tutankhamen's tomb completely intact. It turns out that when another tomb was being built nearby, the builders threw the debris on King Tutankhamen's tomb. His tomb had been completely covered up! When Egyptologists uncovered King Tutankhamen's tomb, they found many treasures. There was a solid gold coffin, a gold mask, and the king's mummified body.

Today, the Valley of the Kings still holds many secrets. Egyptologists are still finding hidden chambers and uncovering many of the mysteries of ancient Egypt. By continuing to examine these tombs, we can learn a lot about the way the pharaohs of ancient Egypt lived and died.

Answer the questions.

1. In what country is the Valley of the Kings?

_____

2. What is a pharaoh?

_____

3. How many pharaohs are buried in the Valley of the Kings?

_____

4. Where were most pharaohs buried before the year 1500 BCE?

_____

5. What are three items that the pharaohs took with them to the afterlife?

_____

6. What were the people who broke into tombs called?

_____

7. Who was the first pharaoh to be buried in the Valley of the Kings?

_____

8. Where were the two places tombs are built in the Valley of the Kings?

_____

9. What were some of the tombs built with to catch tomb raiders?

_____

10. Which king's tomb was discovered completely intact?

_____

11. Why had no one raided King Tutankhamen's tomb?

_____

12. What was found in King Tutankhamen's tomb?

_____

The Night Watch

Did you know that there is a painting so famous that a museum has been designed especially for it? *The Night Watch* by Dutch artist Rembrandt Van Rijn hangs in the Rijksmuseum in Amsterdam. Visitors who would like to see the painting must walk through a long entrance hall filled with stained glass. Hanging on the wall at the end of the hall is the huge painting measuring 11 feet (3.4 m) tall and 14 feet (4.3 m) wide. This painting is so important it even has its own escape hatch on the floor below. This is so the painting can be removed quickly in case of a fire.

Rembrandt painted *The Night Watch* in 1642 during the Baroque era. The Baroque era was a time when artists focused on painting scenes that had a lot of drama and tension. This type of painting is known as oil on canvas because Rembrandt used oil-based paint.

The Night Watch is a picture of eighteen men in the Dutch militia. It was commissioned to hang on the wall of the Dutch Assembly Hall. The painting is unique because it is the first portrait showing people in action. At that time, painters only painted people standing or sitting still. Here, the militiamen are preparing their weapons and getting ready to march.

When Rembrandt completed the painting, it was a huge success. Many other groups began asking for similar paintings. Soon, this new style became extremely popular. Rembrandt focused on light and shadow to highlight certain parts of the painting. This method is called "chiaroscuro." For example, there is a little girl in the middle of the scene of men. There are shadows all around her, but the light is focused on her. This ensures that the girl stands out among all the men.

For many years, people thought that the scene took place at night. That is why it had been nicknamed *The Night Watch*. The real name of the painting was much longer and complicated. In the 1940s, layers of dirt and grime were carefully washed away. This revealed that the painting actually took place during the day.

Vandals have tried to damage the painting three times in history. In 1975, the most damage was done when someone slashed the painting with a knife. The painting was carefully restored, but one cut can still be seen.

Today, *The Night Watch* is considered Rembrandt's most important painting.

Read each statement. Write *true* or *false*.

1. *The Night Watch* is located in the city of Amsterdam. _____

2. Rembrandt was an Italian artist. _____

3. *The Night Watch* is a small painting. _____

4. The painting is so famous it has its own escape hatch. _____

5. The style of painting is called Baroque. _____

6. Baroque paintings didn't have any drama or tension. _____

7. There is a group of militiamen in the painting. _____

8. *The Night Watch* is unique because it is the first
   portrait to show people in action. _____

9. When Rembrandt first completed the painting,
   it wasn't very successful. _____

10. Rembrandt focused on light and shadow in the painting. _____

11. *The Night Watch* is a nickname for the painting. _____

12. After the painting was restored, there was no
    evidence that it had ever been vandalized. _____

Let's Make a Periscope

Have you ever wished you could see around corners or observe something without anyone noticing? This is what periscopes are for. Periscopes are instruments used to see things from a hidden spot. Really they are just a long tube with mirrors inside. The mirrors work by reflecting an image back to the viewer. Submarines use periscopes all the time. They stay submerged in water and extend a periscope up to the surface to look around. This allows them to see an enemy before the enemy sees them. The periscope has been used for spying purposes as far back as the 1400s. Today, they are more advanced, and they often come with prisms instead of mirrors.

Using a periscope is a great way to spy! Are you ready to make one of your own?

You will need:

❑ 2 milk cartons   ❑ Scissors   ❑ Packing tape   ❑ Ruler   ❑ Marker

❑ Double-sided tape   ❑ Glue   ❑ 2 small mirrors of the same size

Step 1: With adult supervision, cut the peaked tops of the milk cartons and wash the cartons out.

Step 2: Tape the cut ends of the two cartons together. Wrap the tape around the seam so that it is sturdy.

Step 3: Measure $\frac{1}{4}$ inch from the top of one side of the cartons and mark the spot with a marker.

Step 4: Trace the outline of the mirror along the milk carton starting from right below your measurement.

Step 5: With adult supervision, cut out the portion you traced. It should be the same size as your mirror.

Step 6: Place the mirror in the hole facing the opening. Allow it to slant at a 45-degree angle. Attach the edges to the inside wall of the carton using double-sided tape.

Step 7: Turn the milk cartons over and work at the bottom. (The side with the hole already cut for the mirror should be facing down.)

Step 8: Measure $\frac{1}{4}$ inch from the bottom and repeat the process used in Step 5. (This hole should be on the bottom, while the hole on the other side should be on top.)

Step 9: Place the second mirror into the second hole in the same manner as the first at a 45-degree angle.

Step 10: Look through one of the holes. Do you see an image? If you only see the inside of the box, you need to adjust the mirrors.

Step 11: Once you can see images, glue the mirrors into position.

Step 12: Test your periscope by hiding below or around the corner and spying on someone!

What's the order? Number the events *1* to *12*.

1. _____ Look through one of the holes. Do you see an image? If you only see the inside of the box, you need to adjust the mirrors.

2. _____ Place the mirror in the hole facing the opening. Allow it to slant at a 45-degree angle. Attach the edges to the inside wall of the carton using double-sided tape.

3. _____ Test your periscope by hiding below or around the corner and spying on someone!

4. _____ Trace the outline of the mirror along the milk carton starting from right below your measurement.

5. _____ With adult supervision, cut the peaked tops of the milk cartons and wash the cartons out.

6. _____ Once you can see images, glue the mirrors into position.

7. _____ Place the second mirror into the second hole in the same manner as the first at a 45-degree angle.

8. _____ Turn the milk cartons over and work at the bottom. (The side with the hole already cut for the mirror should be facing down.)

9. _____ Tape the cut ends of the two cartons together. Wrap the tape around the seam so that it is sturdy.

10. _____ Measure $\frac{1}{4}$ inch from the bottom and repeat the process used in Step 5. (This hole should be on the bottom, while the hole on the other side should be on top.)

11. _____ Measure $\frac{1}{4}$ inch from the top of one side of the cartons and mark the spot with a marker.

12. _____ With adult supervision, cut out the portion you traced. It should be the same size as your mirror.

Life Was Different Back Then

If you lived in ancient Rome, your life would be a lot different from what it is today. There were no cars or buses, and there certainly weren't any electronics. In some other ways, life was very similar to the way we do things today.

In ancient Rome, most mornings started off with a light breakfast that consisted of bread and water. Like today, Romans got dressed and ready to go to school or work. They didn't wear jeans and T-shirts though! They usually wore long robes called togas.

School took place in a one-room schoolhouse. Most girls stayed home to help their mothers with chores. Girls from wealthy families had a private tutor or were allowed to attend public school. Children of different ages studied together. Many of the same subjects we still learn today were taught in ancient Rome. They learned math, writing, history, and philosophy. Unlike today when everyone is allowed to go to school, poor children had to stay home.

Only the men of ancient Rome worked. Like today, they might be farmers, builders, traders, or clothing makers. Others became doctors, lawyers, and teachers. Wealthy people only worked until midday. Poor people had very little time for breaks.

Relaxing and socializing were very important in ancient Rome. After work, men and boys went to public bathhouses. Bathhouses weren't just for bathing. Often, they had a library, gardens, and a gymnasium. Today, most people don't go to bathhouses. Instead, they take a bath in their own home. If they want to socialize, they may go to a park or meet friends at a café.

At 3:00 p.m., ancient Romans headed home for the biggest meal of the day. For poor people, this was usually a bowl of porridge. Wealthy Romans might have up to seven courses of food on special occasions. They ate a Mediterranean diet of fruits, salads, eggs, and fish. Sometimes they ate lamb, pork, geese, or chicken.

The evening was a time for entertainment. Like people today, many Romans listened to music, read, or participated in sports. Sometimes they attended gladiator fights or chariot races. They usually went to bed early, because unlike today, they didn't have electricity. Instead, a family shared a single lamp that burned oil.

Finally, the ancient Romans believed in one religion that had many different gods and goddesses. They set up shrines in their homes and often worshipped in temples. Today, people believe in different religions, and some don't believe in religion at all.

Use words from the word bank to complete each sentence.

bathhouses	breakfast	socializing	room	park	togas
school	participated	gymnasium	shrines	philosophy	midday

1. In ancient Rome, most days started with a light _____.

2. They wore long robes called _____.

3. School took place in a one- _____ schoolhouse.

4. They learned math, writing, history, and _____.

5. Poor children didn't go to _____.

6. Wealthy people only worked until _____.

7. Relaxing and _____ were very important for ancient Romans.

8. After work, boys and men went to _____.

9. In bathhouses, you could find a library, gardens, and a _____.

10. Today, if people want to socialize, they may go to a _____ or a café.

11. Like people today, Romans listened to music, read, or _____ in sports.

12. Ancient Romans set up _____ in their homes.

Shintoism

The word *Shinto* means "way of the gods." Shintoism is the oldest religion in Japan and has millions of followers. No one is exactly sure how or even when Shintoism began. What we do know is that it has been around since at least 1000 BCE.

People who follow Shintoism believe that spirits live in the natural world. These spirits are called "kami." Kami can live in plants, trees, mountains, and animals. The kami want their followers to be happy. Shintoists believe that if the kami are treated well, they will bring health and success to their followers. The most important kami is Amaterasu, the sun goddess. Another important kami is Inari, the producer of rice. Inari is well respected because rice is a very important food in Japan.

Shintoists worship in shrines that have been built in nature. There are more than 80,000 shrines throughout Japan to honor the kami. It is believed that the kami are present in these shrines. Each shrine has an archway called a torii. This archway is built as a symbol of separation between the outside world and the sacred world inside the shrine. Before entering, followers rinse their mouths and wash their hands. This is because purity is an important part of Shintoism. Followers want to be pure before entering this sacred place.

Shinto priests can be male or female. It is their job to lead ceremonies in the shrine. Once the ceremony starts, a bell is used to call to the kami. Followers then offer money or rice. Bowing and clapping are also part of the ceremony. This is how the kami knows they are welcome. Some ceremonies are meant for followers to confess wrongdoing, while others are to pray for health or long life.

Every year, festivals are held to pay respect to the kami. One of the biggest festivals occurs on New Year's when communities gather together at their local shrines with food and drink.

Shintoists also worship in their homes. They have a special shelf called a god-shelf set aside for offerings to the kami. They may place rice, tea, or cakes on the shelf before praying. As part of this ritual, Shintoists also worship their ancestors or former emperors.

There are writings about the kami, but there are no books explaining Shinto beliefs. This is because Shintoism is based more on rituals such as ceremonies, offerings, and worship, rather than on a set of beliefs. Many people who practice Shintoism also practice other religions such as Buddhism.

Draw a line to match each description with the correct term.

1. Means "way of the gods"   a) rice

2. Spirits of the natural world   b) god-shelf

3. If the kami are treated well, they bring this to their followers   c) shrines

4. The sun goddess   d) health and success

5. Inari is the producer of this   e) Amaterasu

6. These are built to worship kami   f) priests

7. The number of shrines built in Japan   g) 80,000

8. The archway to the shrine   h) bowing and clapping

9. Followers do this before entering the shrine   i) torii

10. These people lead ceremonies in the shrine   j) Shinto

11. This is part of a Shinto ceremony   k) kami

12. The name of the shelf set aside for worshipping at home   l) rinse their mouths

Ernest Shackleton's Adventure

Ernest Shackleton was a polar explorer who dreamed of being the first person to reach the South Pole. He had no way of knowing that one of his expeditions would become an amazing story of hope and survival.

Born in Ireland in 1874, Ernest Shackleton always had a sense of adventure. As soon as he was old enough, he joined the merchant navy. In 1901, he joined a British naval officer on a trek to the South Pole. Unfortunately, Shackleton became sick, and they had to turn back. Six years later, he tried again. This time Shackleton got closer than before. He was less than 100 miles (161 km) away when poor weather conditions forced him back.

In 1911, a Norwegian explorer named Roald Amundsen beat Shackleton to the South Pole. Shackleton was devastated, but he did not give up his dream. Instead, he planned to cross the continent of Antarctica by route of the South Pole.

On August 1, 1914, Shackleton and his crew of twenty-seven men boarded a ship called the *Endurance*. They had packed everything they needed for a long journey. This included cans of meat, lanterns, and even a banjo to keep them entertained. They also had enough sled dogs to pull the crew across the ice once they reached Antarctica.

As the *Endurance* entered the Weddell Sea, Shackleton realized he and his crew were in danger. There were icebergs everywhere. Shackleton had to steer his ship carefully through sheets of ice. They were less than 100 miles (161 km) from Antarctica, but they were stuck! The ice closed in around them. They stayed trapped in the ice for ten months. With nothing to do but wait, they passed their time playing cards, singing, and listening to music.

Things continued to get worse. The ice began crunching the ship to pieces and soon it was sinking. Shackleton told his crew to abandon ship. They loaded what they could into lifeboats, including the dogs. Killer whales circled around them, and the men were nearly frozen in their clothes.

Eventually, they reached Elephant Island where most of the crew set up camp. But Shackleton could not rest. He knew he had to find help. He set out again, this time with only five others. They rowed their lifeboat for 800 miles (1,287 km) until they reached a whaling station on South Georgia Island.

Four months after he had left his men on Elephant Island, he returned to rescue them. Shackleton was hailed as a true hero. He led his men through treacherous conditions and saved their lives.

Read each question and circle the correct answer.

1. What type of explorer was Ernest Shackleton?

   a) European   b) polar   c) North American

2. What was Shackleton's dream?

   a) to be the first person to reach the South Pole

   b) to be the first person to reach the North Pole   c) to explore new lands

3. Where was Shackleton born?

   a) Great Britain   b) Antarctica   c) Ireland

4. During Shackleton's second expedition to the South Pole, how close did he get?

   a) less than 10 miles (16.1 km)

   b) less than 100 miles (161 km)   c) less than 1,000 miles (1,609.3 km)

5. Once Shackleton realized he wouldn't be the first to reach the South Pole, what did he do?

   a) set out to cross Antarctica   b) gave up   c) explored another part of the world

6. What kind of animals did Shackleton bring on his expedition?

   a) sled dogs   b) cats   c) elephants

7. What was the name of Shackleton's ship?

   a) *Hope*   b) *Endurance*   c) *Trust*

8. When Shackleton entered the Weddell Sea, what surrounded his ship?

   a) killer whales   b) big waves   c) icebergs

9. How long was the *Endurance* trapped in the ice?

   a) ten weeks   b) ten months   c) one year

10. What eventually happened to the ship?

   a) It sank.   b) It was able to break free from the ice.   c) It is still there.

11. While the men were in the lifeboat, what did they have to worry about?

   a) starving   b) sickness   c) killer whales

12. What was the name of the island where the crew finally landed?

   a) Elephant Island   b) Antarctica   c) Penguin Island

Answer Key

Answers to some of the pages may vary.

Page 5
1. a
2. b
3. b
4. c
5. a
6. b
7. a
8. b
9. a
10. b
11. c
12. b

Page 7
1. She was born in London, England.
2. Goodall wanted to travel to Africa.
3. She met Louis Leakey.
4. Leakey asked Goodall to live alone with the chimpanzees.
5. It was unusual because no one had ever done it before.
6. No, she did not have formal training to be an anthropologist.
7. It helped her because she came up with unique ways to record and research her observations.
8. She gave them names.
9. It took one year to establish trust with the chimpanzees.
10. She offered them bananas.
11. They used tools.
12. She dedicated her life to educating others about her findings.

Page 9
1. *diyas*
2. five
3. New Year
4. lights
5. wealth
6. *rangoli*
7. gifts
8. decorating
9. banished
10. demon
11. underworld
12. evil

Page 11
1. true
2. false
3. true
4. true
5. false
6. false
7. false
8. true
9. false
10. true
11. false
12. true

Page 13
1. Step 11
2. Step 9
3. Step 6
4. Step 12
5. Step 10
6. Step 8
7. Step 4
8. Step 5
9. Step 1
10. Step 3
11. Step 7
12. Step 2

Page 15
1. a
2. b
3. c
4. b
5. a
6. a
7. c
8. a
9. b
10. a
11. b
12. c

Page 17
1. water
2. ice
3. wind
4. ice
5. wind
6. water
7. water
8. ice
9. wind
10. water
11. ice
12. wind

Page 19
1. He was born in India.
2. His followers called him the Buddha.
3. Buddha means "enlightened one."
4. The main idea of Buddhism is to relieve suffering.
5. The highest form of peace and happiness is called nirvana.
6. His teachings are known as the dharma.
7. Reincarnation is the belief that when a person dies he is born again.
8. That person will be rewarded.
9. Buddhists encourage kindness and compassion.
10. The practice of sitting and clearing one's mind is called meditating.
11. The two types of Buddhist temples are pagodas and stupas.
12. The Buddhist practice of worship is called *puja*.

Page 21
1. glass
2. greenhouse
3. gases
4. small
5. rise
6. carbon dioxide
7. global warming
8. hotter
9. melt
10. weather
11. hurricanes
12. crops

Page 23
1. true
2. false
3. true
4. true
5. false
6. false
7. true
8. true
9. false
10. true
11. true
12. false

Page 25
1. right
2. right
3. responsibility
4. responsibility
5. right
6. right
7. responsibility
8. right
9. right
10. responsibility
11. responsibility
12. right

Page 27
1. 1564
2. 1574
3. 1581
4. 1585
5. 1588
6. 1589
7. 1592
8. 1609
9. 1610
10. 1632
11. 1642
12. 1992

Page 29
1. b
2. a
3. c
4. a
5. b
6. a
7. a
8. b
9. a
10. c
11. b
12. a

Page 31
1. Aerobic exercise is the best exercise to keep your heart strong.
2. When you do aerobic exercise, you breathe faster, your heart pumps faster, and you sweat.
3. riding a bike, swimming, ice-skating
4. Having strong muscles helps you lift heavy objects.
5. tug-of-war, pull-ups, pushups
6. When you exercise your bones become stronger.
7. If we don't exercise, our muscles tighten as we get older.
8. yoga, gymnastics, martial arts
9. They can put you in a better mood.
10. Endorphins are the chemical that is released when you exercise.
11. Endorphins make you happier.
12. Having an active lifestyle helps prevent disease.

Page 33
1. L'Shanah Tova
2. synagogue
3. world
4. Rosh Hashanah
5. reflection
6. forgiveness
7. work
8. *Shofar*
9. 100
10. *Tashlich*
11. Bread
12. circle

Page 35
1. b
2. a
3. c
4. a
5. b
6. c
7. a
8. c
9. a
10. b
11. b
12. a

Page 37
1. true
2. false
3. true
4. false
5. true
6. true
7. true
8. false
9. false
10. true
11. true
12. false

Page 39

1. Hungary
2. five
3. shoes
4. magic
5. nickname
6. assistant
7. Chicago
8. newspaper
9. escape artist
10. cuffed
11. famous
12. fifty-two

Page 41

1. James Naismith invented basketball.
2. A soccer ball was used for the first basketball game.
3. Regulation hoops are 10 feet (3 m) high.
4. A regulation court is 94 feet (28.7 m) long.
5. This is called a half-court game.
6. You can improvise with boxes or a bucket.
7. A full-court game requires ten players.
8. The team with the ball is called the offense.
9. The three-point line is 20 feet (6.1 m) from the hoop.
10. No, once you stop dribbling, you cannot start again.
11. This is called a chest pass.
12. A ball can bounce once during a bounce pass.

Page 43

1. c
2. a
3. a
4. b
5. c
6. a
7. b
8. b
9. a
10. c
11. a
12. c

Page 45

1. h
2. i
3. j
4. c
5. d
6. e
7. k
8. f
9. g
10. l
11. a
12. b

Page 47

1. Africa
2. 30
3. tributaries
4. Blue
5. Sudan
6. fertile
7. mud
8. papyrus
9. floods
10. stone
11. 12,000 (3,657.6 m)
12. riverboat

Page 49

1. false
2. false
3. true
4. true
5. true
6. false
7. false
8. true
9. false
10. false
11. true
12. false

Page 51

1. A person being bullied might feel alone or scared.
2. A person being bullied might have a hard time focusing.
3. A person being bullied might have low self-esteem.
4. The best way to prevent bullying is to respect one another.
5. Before saying something mean, a person should stop and think.
6. A good way to lighten the situation is to respond with a joke.
7. If your feelings are hurt you should speak to an adult.
8. Three people who can help stop the bullying from continuing are a teacher, an adult, and a parent.
9. No, it is not a good idea to think about revenge.
10. You should surround yourself with friends.
11. If someone is bullying you on a bus, you should sit closer to the bus driver.
12. You should walk with confidence.

Page 53

1. b
2. a
3. a
4. b
5. b
6. c
7. a
8. c
9. a
10. c
11. b
12. a

Page 55

1. honors
2. celebration
3. holiday
4. spread
5. busy
6. ornaments
7. attend
8. choose
9. considered
10. exchange
11. declared
12. buy

Page 57

1. Step 11
2. Step 9
3. Step 5
4. Step 12
5. Step 1
6. Step 8
7. Step 2
8. Step 6
9. Step 4
10. Step 7
11. Step 3
12. Step 10

Page 59

1. true
2. false
3. true
4. true
5. true
6. false
7. false
8. true
9. true
10. false
11. true
12. false

Page 61

1. h
2. a
3. g
4. c
5. k
6. j
7. f
8. d
9. i
10. e
11. l
12. b

Page 63

1. 1884
2. 1892
3. 1894
4. 1905
5. 1914
6. 1921
7. 1933
8. 1935
9. 1945
10. 1948
11. 1953
12. 1962

Page 65

1. feeling
2. Everybody
3. presentation
4. tasks
5. time
6. sick
7. problems
8. list
9. after-school
10. sleep
11. sugar
12. Exercise

Page 67

1. streak
2. specific gravity
3. cleavage
4. luster
5. hardness
6. fracture
7. specific gravity
8. luster
9. hardness
10. fracture
11. streak
12. cleavage

Page 69

1. Ancient Mesopotamia is known as the cradle of civilization.
2. The part of the world where ancient Mesopotamia was located is now called southern Iraq.
3. They first began to settle this area because of the fertile lands.
4. It was necessary so that they could write down information.
5. The head of Sumerian society was the king.
6. Priests were also doctors.
7. Laborers and farmers made up the lower class.
8. The Sumerians captured slaves during battles.
9. Houses were made from mud bricks.
10. They sometimes slept on their roofs.
11. They used sheepskin or wool to make clothing.
12. During festive occasions, drums, flutes, and harps were used.

Page 71

1. a
2. b
3. b
4. a
5. c
6. a
7. c
8. a
9. b
10. c
11. a
12. c

Page 73
1. Step 11
2. Step 8
3. Step 12
4. Step 6
5. Step 10
6. Step 2
7. Step 4
8. Step 1
9. Step 5
10. Step 7
11. Step 3
12. Step 9

Page 75
1. water
2. surface
3. pushes
4. Canada
5. Tidal
6. moon
7. sediment
8. Deep water
9. saltiness
10. heat
11. warm
12. climate

Page 77
1. true
2. false
3. true
4. false
5. true
6. true
7. false
8. true
9. false
10. true
11. false
12. true

Page 79
1. least
2. unprepared
3. leaving
4. carefree
5. weak
6. bitter
7. last
8. refusal
9. old
10. ordinary
11. disagree
12. bad

Page 81
1. c
2. a
3. b
4. a
5. c
6. a
7. b
8. a
9. b
10. c
11. a
12. b

Page 83
1. The Valley of the Kings is in Egypt.
2. A pharaoh is a ruler.
3. More than sixty pharaohs are buried in the Valley of Kings.
4. Before 1500 BCE, most pharaohs were buried in pyramids.
5. Answers will vary but may include: cookware, preserved food, jewels, and carvings.
6. People who broke into tombs were called tomb raiders.

7. The first pharaoh to be buried in the Valley of the Kings was King Thutmose I.
8. Tombs were built in a mountainside and the valley floor.
9. They were built with trap doors.
10. King Tutankhamen's tomb was discovered intact.
11. It had been covered up.
12. Inside King Tutankhamen's tomb was a gold mask, a gold coffin, and his mummified body.

Page 85
1. true
2. false
3. false
4. true
5. false
6. false
7. true
8. true
9. false
10. true
11. true
12. false

Page 87
1. Step 10
2. Step 6
3. Step 12
4. Step 4
5. Step 1
6. Step 11
7. Step 9
8. Step 7
9. Step 2
10. Step 8
11. Step 3
12. Step 5

Page 89
1. breakfast
2. togas
3. room
4. philosophy
5. school
6. midday
7. socializing
8. bathhouses
9. gymnasium
10. park
11. participated
12. shrines

Page 91
1. j
2. k
3. d
4. e
5. a
6. c
7. g
8. i
9. l
10. f
11. h
12. b

Page 93
1. b
2. a
3. c
4. b
5. a
6. a
7. b
8. c
9. b
10. a
11. c
12. a

Image Credits